RUGBY'S STRANGEST MATCHES

Also in the same series

Cricket's Strangest Matches by Andrew Ward
Horse-Racing's Strangest Races by Andrew Ward
Boxing's Strangest Fights by Graeme Kent
Football's Strangest Matches by Andrew Ward
Golf's Strangest Rounds by Andrew Ward

RUGBY'S STRANGEST MATCHES

Extraordinary but true stories from
over a century of rugby

John Griffiths

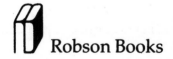 Robson Books

First published in Great Britain in 2000 by Robson Books,
10 Blenheim Court, Brewery Road, London N7 9NT

A member of the Chrysalis Group plc

A catalogue record for this title is available from the British
Library

ISBN 1 86105 354 1

Printed and bound in Great Britain by Creative Print & Design
(Wales), Ebbw Vale

CONTENTS

INTRODUCTION

Rugby's Strangest Matches describes some of the game's most curious occasions of the past 130 years. Any unusual team or individual performance, or any occurrence during or surrounding a match that was a clear departure from the normal run of things, has been regarded as strange and thus worthy of inclusion.

This collection of true stories includes the match when an Irish international player arranged his marriage in order to qualify for leave of absence to play against England, the occasion when a team of top English soccer players beat their rugby counterparts at the fifteen-a-side game, the game where an almost complete unknown played for his country due to an administrative mistake, and the match where a well-known referee was sent off.

Naturally, 'strangeness' is subjective depending on the circumstances at the time and one's own point of view. Therefore there may well be some argument relating to what has been included and what has been left out. For the most part, the stories concentrate on the games played at senior international level because these attracted more attention and wider media coverage. No doubt there are many others which would qualify for inclusion, but for which there are no reported accounts.

The majority of the work is based on newspaper research and personal memories. My first debt of gratitude is therefore to the recorders of the game, past and present, for setting down what otherwise would have been lost for all time. In particular, the personal recollections and lighter asides, in word and in print, of Ian Malin, David Hands, John Mason, Steve Jones, Rob

Wildman, Brendan Gallagher, Frank Keating, Patrick Lennon and Mick Cleary have helped to illuminate many of the stories appearing in this collection.

In addition, my thanks go to Vivian Jenkins, arguably the game's best-informed writer of all time, who provided memories from the more distant past. As player, journalist and spectator, Viv has witnessed most of the more important matches of the past 75 years. A peerless story-teller, this book could have been filled by his rugby recollections alone.

Elsewhere, behind the scenes, I owe a debt of gratitude to three old friends, Tim Auty of Leeds, Geoff Miller in New Zealand and Tony Lewis of Pyle in South Wales for suggesting ideas and forwarding copies of cuttings from their own archives. Finally, thanks go to Jeremy Robson for commissioning this title, and to Lorna Russell at Robson Books for her skilful and patient management of the project.

DR ALMOND'S WORDS OF WISDOM

EDINBURGH, MARCH 1871

Rugby union's first international was always going to be a strange match. The background to the occasion gives some insight into the unusual circumstances surrounding international sport nearly 130 years ago.

There had been a soccer international between England and a 'Scotland XI' in November 1870. England's win by a goal to nil angered those north of the Border, where it was contended that the only connection the losers had with 'their' country was a liking for Scotch whisky. The Scots asserted that the principal version of football played at their schools and universities was rugby and they issued a challenge to England to pick a side for an international rugby match to be staged at Raeburn Place, Edinburgh, in March 1871.

The English accepted and their selected 20 (13 forwards and seven backs) got down to earnest preparations for the big match. Typical of the training undertaken by their players was the regimen of one John Henry Clayton, a forward from the Liverpool club. Weighing in at more than 17-stone, his training makes fascinating reading. For a month before the match he ran four miles every morning, his large Newfoundland dog 'making the pace'. A four-mile horseback ride took him to his Liverpool office where he put in a twelve-hour day, 8 a.m. to 8 p.m., before making the return journey home to a dinner of underdone-beef-and-beer. He laid claim to a 'frugal and strenuous life otherwise'.

Travelling arrangements were in stark contrast to those of

today. England travelled north on Saturday night (for the Monday match) in third-class rail carriages with bare board seats. Arriving at dawn next day, they took baths before finding accommodation. All travelling and hotel expenses were met by the players themselves.

The next day dawned bright and clear and more than 2000 spectators arrived to see Scotland win on a pitch that was judged narrow compared with English standards. The game was largely a protracted maul – imagine rugby today being played among 40 men, most of them forwards – and several of the laws peculiar to the Scottish version of rugby were adopted. England, in short, were clearly playing against the odds. Even so, in the two halves of 50 minutes each, their backs impressed Scottish observers with their willingness to run with the ball.

Scoring by points was not introduced to rugby football until the late 1880s and at the time of this inaugural international the only way a match could be won was by a majority of goals: drop goals or converted tries. (Penalty goals would not sully rugby's scoring until more than 20 years later.) Tries alone were of no value. They simply enabled sides to 'try' for a goal.

Scotland scored the only goal of the match early in the second half. They succeeded in pushing a scrummage over the England goal line and to Angus Buchanan, who grounded the ball, fell the distinction of scoring the first try in international rugby. But not before England had disputed its legality.

A lengthy and by all accounts heated debate ensued before the try was allowed to stand. Referees did not appear in matches until the mid-1870s so appeals were heard by umpires (later known as touch judges). The umpire who awarded the try, which was converted into a goal by William Cross with a fine kick, was Scotland's Dr Almond, the well-known headmaster of Loretto.

The wisdom behind his allowing the score was later set in print: 'Let me make a confession,' he wrote. 'I do not know whether the decision which gave Scotland the try from which the winning goal was kicked was correct in fact. When an umpire is in doubt, I think he is justified in deciding against the side which makes most noise. They are probably in the wrong.'

Both sides added later tries but in the absence of successful conversions, Scotland held their controversial lead. Accounts of the match refer to their superior fitness so it seems reasonable to assume that the better side won.

DOG BITES RUGBY PLAYER

CAMBRIDGE, FEBRUARY 1873

Parker's Piece, Cambridge, in the 1870s was a million miles from the Twickenham of the 1990s packed with 70,000 spectators watching the senior universities contest the Bowring Bowl. But the famous old cricket ground has great significance in rugby union's history for it was here in the 1840s that the first senior rugby outside the public schools was played. A club had been formed at the University as early as 1839 by Arthur Pell, who later became MP for Leicester.

Parker's Piece was, moreover, the venue for the second University rugby match when Oxford turned up there two players short in February 1873. It was also a perilous venue for one of the Oxford pack, George Podmore. During the match, which Cambridge won by a goal and two tries to nil, he was bitten by a stray dog.

IRISH CHAOS

THE OVAL, FEBRUARY 1875

Ireland's entry into international rugby in 1875 was surrounded by chaos. The Irish Football Union was formed in November the previous year but, much to the annoyance of the Belfast rugby clubs, none of their representatives were present. That same month in Belfast, a representative Dublin club rugby XV played their Belfast counterparts in a forerunner of what is now the Leinster-Ulster inter-provincial matches. There was great interest in the match, as it was perceived as a trial for the forthcoming international against England.

The Belfast men triumphed in difficult conditions and then proceeded to give the vanquished a wigging. The Ulstermen underlined their annoyance at not having been invited to the formation of the Union by proceeding to form their own North of Ireland Union in direct opposition to the Dubliners.

However, with the fixture against England in London looming, the two parties eventually reached a compromise. It was diplomatically decided that both should nominate ten players to the team of 20. But not much thought went into the selection process.

There was no communication between the two unions about the positions players would occupy. Indeed, many of them had never seen one another before. As a result, there was chaos. Backs were made to play in forward positions and vice-versa. Two of those chosen to play did not even appear and it was no surprise that Ireland were penned deep in their own half for the entire match.

The trenchant Irish critic of the day, Jacques MacCarthy, wrote: 'The whole lot were immaculately innocent of training.' They were also unfit and, it was reckoned, would have been well beaten by a fourth-rate London club. In fairness, it should be pointed out that rugby in Ireland in the 1870s was played by teams of 15-a-side and the Irish forwards who met England at the Oval were far too light and inexperienced to play effectively at the long-drawn-out mauling game that was a feature of 20-a-side rugby.

Ireland were also found wanting in the drop-kicking department. The technique was virtually unknown in their club circles and when Richard Walkington, their full-back, was entrusted with a drop-out he was unable to propel the ball farther than ten yards.

Even so, despite their inadequacies, Ireland only went down by a goal, a dropped goal and a try to nil. That, however, did not prevent the football correspondent of the *Field* from declaring: 'I could whip up twenty Irishmen resident in London who would make hares of this pseudo-Irish twenty.'

THE FIRST FIFTEENS

THE OVAL, FEBRUARY 1877

Those who turned up to see the international match between England and Ireland in 1877 would have regarded the events of the next 80 minutes as quite unusual.

Up to this time, internationals had been played between teams of 20 players a side, normally lined out with three full-backs, a solitary threequarter back, three half-backs and 13 forwards. Most of the time the ball was lost in scrums and mauls comprising 26 forwards. Backs would have been very lucky to get their hands on the ball and attacking movements among them were virtually non-existent.

On the rare occasions when a player was able to make a run with the ball, one of the vast number of opponents invariably collared him. The laws of the game at the time required a player so held to call 'Down'. That was the signal for the two packs to gather around the player, who then placed the ball on the floor. A scrum then formed around the ball and the object was for one set of forwards to try to drive it through and break away down field, usually with a dribble.

Such scrums were protracted affairs because there was no heeling or wheeling. Sides coming away with the ball left opponents lying on the ground in their wake. Brawn rather than brain was the order of the day.

Mindful that the rugby held little spectacle for anybody other than those who had played it, the law-making authorities began experimenting with ways to speed up the game. In 1875, Oxford and Cambridge pioneered the 15-a-side game and 15 months later the reduced number was first adopted for inter-national matches when England hosted Ireland at Kennington Oval, home of the Surrey Cricket Club.

'The ball naturally made its appearance sooner from the diminished number of forwards, though the scrummages were still of formidable length owing to the methods then employed,' it was noted, after England had beaten the Irish by two goals and two tries to nil.

The England team was a light combination, selected, per-haps, with the 15-a-side occasion in mind. They were nimbler to the ball than their rivals and, observed the rugby corre-spondent of *The Times*, 'knew more of the science of the game.'

The match was the first in which Albert Hornby, the Lancashire Test cricketer, appeared in an England rugby jersey. Aged nearly 30, he was the first rugby player to make use of the punt as a device for gaining ground. His kicks were an innovation as far as international rugby was concerned at the time and his effective methods attracted considerable comment.

Hornby had attended Harrow School where, it was reported, the football game practised in his day was quite different from the version at Rugby School. The original Harrow game did not admit drop-kicking; indeed, the shape of the football was unsuited to such kicking. In its place, Hornby had developed the technique of punting and it was this kicking style which made him conspicuous throughout the match.

For the spectator in 1877, then, international rugby must have appeared to be a whole new ball game, with that year's England-Ireland fixture clearly marking the beginning of its modern version.

AND THERE WAS LIGHT

BROUGHTON, OCTOBER 1878

In the late 1870s bids were mounted by the fledgling electrical light companies to overturn the monopoly the gas companies held over urban street lighting. As Thomas Edison, in the United States, and Sir Joseph Swan, in Britain, perfected the design of the incandescent light bulb, less inspired experimenters were already using more primitive forms of electrical lighting.

Sport was an interested beneficiary of the new form of lighting with both football and rugby pioneering floodlit events in the winter of 1878–9. The first recorded rugby match under floodlights took place in the industrial north when Broughton entertained Swinton on 22 October, 1878. Two Gramme's Lights suspended from 30-foot poles were used for illumination. Another match was staged in the Liverpool area the same month and the craze for 'illuminated matches' spread like wildfire as the electrical companies sought to promote their methods.

An interesting additional development in November was the use of a white ball for a match staged at Old Deer Park involving Surrey and Middlesex. Surrey won a match enlightened by four lamps driven by a couple of Siemens electro-dynamo machines.

Three months later on 24 February, 1879, the first floodlit game in Scotland took place at Hawick. Their local derby with Melrose, whom they defeated by a goal to nil, attracted a healthy crowd of 5000 and a gate of £63. (It would have been much greater but for the fact that only one gate man was on duty and many poured through a hole in a perimeter fence without paying.) The power for the light came from two dynamos driven by steam engines, but the crowd had a shock when the parsimonious officials switched the power off immediately the match finished. Heavy snow had covered the pitch and surrounds and there was chaos as spectators skidded their way home in complete darkness.

Floodlit rugby for gate-money was actually prohibited by the Rugby Football Union 'as not in the interests of the game' in 1933. By the 1950s, however, Harlequins and Cardiff were staging a popular sequence of annual evening matches at the White City (before the Quins set up home at the Stoop) and there was a successful Floodlit Alliance series involving the major Welsh clubs in the 1960s.

Nowadays major internationals in the southern hemisphere are frequently staged as night games and the official world record attendance for a rugby union match was set when Australia played the All Blacks under the lights of the Olympic Stadium, Sydney, in July 2000. A crowd of 109,874 turned out to see the New Zealanders win a pulsating match 39–35.

LUCKY TO GET NIL

BLACKHEATH, FEBRUARY 1881

When the successful Welsh sides of the late 1960s and 1970s regularly beat England, and quite often by large scores, the joke in Wales was that the fixture would be dropped the next season – the implication being that England were unworthy of a full international match with mighty Wales.

Perhaps the Welsh were trying to get their own back for a slight against them by England nearly a hundred years earlier, when the sides first met in 1881 in one of the oddest matches ever involving Wales. It was a game that marked their entry into international rugby and took place before even the Welsh Rugby Union itself had been founded.

The man known as the 'father of Welsh Rugby', Richard Mullock, was the inspiration behind their maiden inter-national. A mover and shaker of the South Wales Football Union, Mullock wrote to the Rugby Football Union in London early in the 1880–81 season, proposing an international rugby match with England. The English accepted the challenge and arranged a fixture for 19 February 1881 at Richardson's Field, Blackheath, which was then home to the famous Blackheath club.

If enterprise was one of Mr Mullock's strengths, organisation certainly wasn't. No trial match was staged and players were eventually chosen for the match by virtue of reputation. One of the last survivors of that Welsh side was Major Richard Summers of Haverfordwest. In an interview many years later he recalled that he was informally asked to play on the strength of

11

his performances a couple of years earlier for his school, Cheltenham College, in matches against Cardiff and Newport.

No formal invitations to play were sent out to the Welsh XV. Two of those expected to appear in the side did not turn up because they had not received instructions to attend and two bystanders, University undergraduates with tenuous Welsh links but who had travelled to London to see the match, had to be roped in to play for their country.

Mullock, however, did have the inspiration of clothing his side in scarlet jerseys and chose the Prince of Wales feathers as the emblem. Researchers have never uncovered his reasons for veering away from the black shirts with white leek that identified the uniform of the South Wales Football Club, the prototypes of representative Welsh rugby.

The Blackheath club used a local hostelry on the heath (the Princess of Wales, which remains a popular pub to this day) as its meeting and changing point for matches at the time. So, after mustering at the pub, the players of both countries changed and walked the half-mile or so across the Common to play.

The game was a farce. The Welsh were hopelessly outplayed and must have over-indulged earlier whilst at the pub, for they went down by the staggering margin of seven goals, six tries and a dropped goal to nil. (82–0 under modern scoring values.) 'We were lucky to get nil,' said one of the Welsh team afterwards.

The Rugby Football Union were clearly unimpressed by the visitors. They *did* drop the fixture the following season, a glance through the record books showing that the Welsh only played against the North of England at Newport in January of the 1881–2 season. By then, though, the fall-out from the Blackheath disaster had led to Welsh rugby putting its house into some sort of order. The Union officially came into force in March 1881 and, although beaten at Newport, 'the good form shown by the Welshmen,' it was written, 'gained for them a place in the International fixtures [with England] of the future.'

THE LONG DISPUTED TRY

BLACKHEATH, MARCH 1884

The 1884 season was the first in which all four of the Home Unions played against each other. The Championship title depended on a head-on collision between the year's two unbeaten sides, England and Scotland, at Blackheath in March.

More than 8,000 made the trip to south-east London to see Scotland take the lead with a first half try that was not converted. Soon after the interval came a disputed try. Scotland won a scrum near their line but one of their forwards, Charles Berry, fumbled the ball and knocked it backwards. Charles Gurdon picked it up for England, made a bee-line for the posts and fed it to fellow forward Richard Kindersley, who plunged over the line to claim a try.

The Scots, however, made an appeal to the referee that the try be disallowed. (Appeals by teams were part and parcel of the game in the 1880s.) They contended that *their* knock back had been illegal. But in England knock backs were perfectly legal and the point made by the English players to the referee, George Scriven of Ireland, was that in any case it was unfair that Scotland should benefit by their own mistake. (The rule relating to advantage did not enter the law book for another dozen years.) After ten minutes of earnest discussion, the referee ruled in England's favour and Wilfrid Bolton kicked the goal that sealed the match and with it the Championship.

After the game the Scots steadfastly refused to accept the ruling. The root of the problem was a straightforward

13

difference in the reading of the laws, but why, they contended, should the Rugby Football Union (RFU) have sole rights over interpretation. The RFU's defence was more to the point: they argued that whatever the interpretation, the referee's decision was final.

But the two nations remained at loggerheads and cancelled their fixture for 1885. A year later the Irish Rugby Union proposed the formation of an International Board to frame the laws of the game and make rulings on disputes. Scotland and Wales were party to a meeting in Dublin where the Scots, two years after the event, finally accepted the outcome of their 1884 game.

England, unhappy about representation, boycotted the early meetings of the Board. In 1887 the Celtic nations passed a vote that effectively cold-shouldered the English from the International Championship for two years and it was not until 1890 that differences were finally resolved and England returned to the fold.

The International Board has remained rugby's leading administrative body ever since, but it is interesting to reflect that it might never have come into being but for Scotland's objections in that 1884 game with England.

ONE-ARMED PLAYER'S RECORD

NEWTON ABBOT, JANUARY 1886

When a player named Wakeham kicked 13 conversions from 13 attempts for Newton Abbot against Plymouth on 30 January 1886 it was claimed as a record for a club match in England.

The mark has long since been overtaken but one astonishing fact regarding Wakeham renders his record remarkable to this day: he had only one arm.

PLAYED TWO, LOST TWO, TRIES CONCEDED 15

CARDIFF/EDINBURGH, JANUARY 1886/FEBRUARY 1887

Wales had been playing international rugby for only four years when they first held the Scots (with more than a decade of Test play under their belts) to a nil-all draw in Glasgow in 1885. When the Welsh XV prepared for the next match against Scotland, at Cardiff in January 1886, they were optimistic that they would collect their first win of the series. The match, however, turned out to be the first part of a disastrous Welsh two-act play in the series against Scotland.

A curiosity of the 1886 game was that for the first time an international XV (Wales) chose to field four threequarters and only eight forwards. The experiment was thrust on the Welsh side as a result of its successful innovation at club level two years earlier by Cardiff RFC.

The chief proponent of the new system was Frank Hancock, the Cardiff captain, who came in to captain the Welsh XV with a brief to oversee the introduction of the Cardiff idea at national level.

But the system did not translate successfully to international level. Wales were overrun in the first half and conceded three tries. At half-time big Harry Bowen, the Llanelli full-back, was moved up to bolster a pack that had been completely out-scrummaged in the tight. But this was too little too late. Wales lost by three tries to nil. For the next encounter with the Scots, 13 months later in Edinburgh, Wales reverted to the nine forwards and three threequarters formation in the hope of reversing the result.

Disaster was again the outcome, but this time on an even grander scale. Wales crashed to a twelve try defeat, with Scotland's George Lindsay scoring five tries, a record that still stands for an International Championship match. Wales had thus conceded 15 tries against the Scots in two matches.

So what would come next? Suprisingly, the first Welsh win of the series. It came out of the blue twelve months later when the London Welsh wing Tom Pryce Jenkins hared along the touchline at Rodney Parade, Newport, and won the match with the only score of the game.

IS A DOG A SPECTATOR?

PORTSMOUTH, NOVEMBER 1886

The early rugby handbooks provide fascinating insights into the laws of the game in series of space-fillers under the heading of points often enquired about. One such query relates to a match played between Portsmouth Victoria and Southampton Trojans in November 1886.

During the match the ball was kicked into the Trojans' in-goal area where it rebounded off a stray dog. One of the Victoria players gathered it and touched down to claim a try. The Trojans protested, claiming that the referee should have ruled 'dead ball' the ball having struck 'a spectator'.

The objection was later referred to the Rugby Football Union whose committee ruled that the try should stand, as dogs were not classed as spectators.

A HEROIC ACT

DUBLIN, FEBRUARY 1887

International rugby has been played on Lansdowne Road, Dublin, since 1878, making it the oldest arena in the world still staging Test matches.

It is always worth travelling a long way to experience the *craic* at the ground, whether Ireland win or lose, and one of the earliest days when the good-natured Irish had one of their own famous victories to enjoy was in early February 1887, when they defeated England for the first time.

The match was Ireland's opening game of the International Championship and, according to the critics of the day, their determination to give a good account of themselves against a team that had registered eleven wins and a draw in the opening dozen matches of rugby union's second-oldest international series, was never greater.

Ireland selected a team that was the customary mix of youth and experience. Six of the chosen XV were former internationals, including their captain and half-back, Robert Warren. Among the new caps was big John Macauley, a forward, and Dolway Walkington, of whom it was said: 'in the dark his delicate sight tells terribly against him.' Fortunately for him the weather in Dublin on that February day was bright and clear and Walkington is reported to have enjoyed a blinder, playing his part in defence to keep Ireland's line intact against an England side that had lost only twice in the previous ten years.

For Macauley, however, taking part in the game did not prove so straightforward. A miller's agent in Limerick, he had already used up his quota of holidays for the working year when he was called up for this match and consequently was refused further time off to play in the match. But Macauley was determined to take part and resorted to the only means left to him. He took the unusual step of getting married in order to obtain the necessary leave of absence. According to an Irish critic of the day: 'This was truly heroic, and his wife fully endorsed the enthusiasm.'

This heroism was amply rewarded. Ireland won by two converted tries to nil. English reports of the game were written in a tone that almost bordered on condescension. The blame for England's defeat was placed firmly on their forwards for 'allowing themselves to be hustled all over the field by their opponents'. The Irish, however, were ecstatic at beating England 'all ends up'.

Macauley himself maintained a lifelong interest in Irish rugby up to the time of his death in his nineties in 1958. He served the Irish Rugby Union as its president in 1894–5, but his course of action in order to play in that match of 1877 does not seem to have been an inspiration to other Irish rugby players of the time. Up to the outbreak of war in 1914, only four married men had appeared in an Ireland rugby jersey.

There is, though, a tantalisingly cryptic comment on this match in the writings of Jacques MacCarthy, the Irish rugby writer whose reflections quite often appeared to be of the don't-let-the-facts-spoil-a-good-story school of journalism.

Reminiscing five years after the match, MacCarthy revealed: 'There are secrets about this match which must remain for the instruction of a future generation,' although he did divulge further that: 'Everything was arranged cut and dry, even to the very ball that was played with.'

Possibly the Irish met a day before the match to run through some tactics. In the 1880s, such an action would have been tantamount to an act of professionalism. Certainly the match reports of the game refer to the discipline of the well-drilled Irish forwards. But no-one seems to have put in print the real story behind this match.

TIME GENTLEMEN PLEASE?

WAKEFIELD, JANUARY 1889

Yorkshire were declared winners of the inaugural official English county championship in 1888–9. The county carried all before them that winter, winning all six of their matches against other counties. They also played twice against the touring New Zealand Natives that season.

For the first match against the visitors at Manningham in December, the county made a huge error of judgement in fielding what effectively amounted to a second XV and were well beaten by the Natives. For the return match at Wakefield a month later, the full strength of the county was called on to restore Yorkshire pride. William Cail, later a president and long-serving treasurer to the Rugby Football Union, acted as referee.

The county avenged its earlier defeat with a handsome victory over the tourists, but it was Mr Cail, with an episode of high farce, who provided the lasting memory of the match.

He had stopped his watch as usual when one of the Natives' forwards went down injured. After the player was passed fit to resume, however, poor Cail forgot to re-set his watch. It was twenty or so minutes later that, sensing the match must be drawing to its close, he next glanced at his watch only to discover to his horror that it had stopped. He immediately called a halt to the game and dashed up into the press seats to appeal for an accurate measure regarding the time that had elapsed before returning to the pitch and resuming the game.

21

The crowd, content that their side had won comfortably (it might well have been different otherwise) found this very amusing. 'No less amusing,' it was later divulged, 'were the different replies made by the pressmen.'

A MAORI PROTEST

BLACKHEATH, FEBRUARY 1889

The tour of the 1888–9 New Zealand Native team was the most demanding in the game's history. The side, all of whom were native-born players, was known as the Maoris, although not all of them were full-blooded Maori. The playing party numbered 26 and assembled in May 1888 for a journey to Britain via Melbourne and Suez. The original itinerary took in a staggering 50-plus matches spread over six months. But, by the time the party broke up more than a year later, 107 matches had been played in England, Scotland, Ireland, Wales, Australia and New Zealand. Of these, 78 were won, six drawn and only 23 lost. In addition, the team played eight Aussie Rules matches during its three-week stay in Melbourne.

The British section of the tour opened in October with a match against Surrey County. In its preview of the match, the *Daily Telegraph*, long before the days of political correctness, told its readers, 'The Maoris have progressed since Captain Cook found the neatly tattooed ancestors of our visitors eating each other in the bush.'

The tourists won handsomely before a crowd numbering some 5000, which included most of the touring Australian cricketers who had a month or so earlier lost the Ashes series to an England side led by Dr W G Grace. The match was refereed by Rowland Hill, the secretary of the Rugby Football Union, and as the game had passed uneventfully, the tourists took with a pinch of salt the warnings of the Aussie cricketers that they could expect difficulties with English referees.

Those warnings would haunt the Maoris four months later during the international against England at Blackheath. The referee for the match was again Rowland Hill, but this time the match was far from uneventful.

Play was even for the first quarter but, before half-time, England scored two tries in controversial circumstances. Billy Warbrick, the Maoris' full-back, began to run with the ball from his own in-goal area after a wayward kick by an England player had almost sent the ball dead. Harry Bedford, one of the England forwards, followed up and put pressure on Warbrick who decided to touch down. As he touched down, Bedford threw himself at the ball and, to the dismay of the visitors, the referee awarded a try to England. Before the interval, Bedford had scored another try in similar circumstances after Harry Lee, one of the Maori forwards, had claimed a touch down after a maul in goal.

The tourists were pretty despondent when they turned round two tries behind at the break, but their annoyance was as nothing compared with the pandemonium that broke out after an England score in the second half.

Andrew Stoddart, one of the English threequarters (and the last man to captain England at both rugby football and cricket), made a dash along the touchline and seemed set for a try when his shorts were torn in a tackle made by Tom Ellison, one of the Maoris' best players. The players formed the customary guard around Stoddart while he waited for a new pair of pants. In the meantime, the referee allowed play to continue and, to the distress of the tourists, Frank Evershed for England picked up the ball and proceeded to cross unchallenged for a try that John Sutcliffe converted into a goal in his only international rugby appearance. (He was, however, another dual England international who kept goal for Plymouth Argyle, Bolton Wanderers and five times for England.)

Three of the disgusted Native side walked off in protest at this point and for a while the referee allowed the match to continue with England playing against only 12 men. Eventually the New Zealanders' manager persuaded his men to return but

England finished comfortable winners.

English rugby had never witnessed such a demonstration as this in an international match and rebukes for the Maoris' reactions were swift in coming. The Union demanded an instant apology from the Maoris. That Rowland Hill, their secretary, had been the referee involved no doubt compounded the insult to the Union over the Maori walk-off.

An apology was forthcoming, but was not deemed adequate enough by the high-minded Union officials, who threatened to effectively cancel the remainder of the tour by forbidding their clubs from playing the tourists. In the end, the tourists had to eat humble pie and Edward McCausland, who had led them in the international, wrote a second apology to Rowland Hill: 'I beg to apologise to the Rugby Union committee for the insults offered by my team to their officials on the field of play on Saturday last.'

The apology had been dictated to the New Zealanders by none other than Hill himself. Nor did the coolness of the Union to the Maoris end there. When the tourists returned to London later in the tour they were socially ignored. Moreover, the tourists received no official send-off when they departed Britain in April.

DÉJÀ VU

Joseph Jameson must have thought that he was seeing things when he lined up in the Ireland XV to face England at Manchester in February 1892. Either that or he had partaken the night before of one glass too many of the famous whiskey that bore his name.

The reason for his confusion was one James Marsh, now standing before him in the white jersey and red rose of England. Hadn't this same James Marsh stood before him almost three years earlier at the Ballynafeigh Grounds in Belfast . . . playing in the navy blue of Scotland?

Poor Jameson's feelings of déjà vu were not the results of any trickery. He was absolutely right in his reading of matters. This was the very same Marsh whose punting and tackling had played a part in Ireland's downfall by a dropped goal to nil in Belfast in 1889. Marsh, who appeared in the threequarter line, was a former Edinburgh Institute pupil who qualified in medicine from Edinburgh University.

He won two caps for Scotland before settling in general practice in the Manchester area. As a young man he joined the Swinton club and his strong all-round play came to the attention of the England selectors, who named him as a centre for the annual North versus South match in 1890–1. The following season he won his sole cap helping England to beat Ireland 7–0.

The immediate upshot of his playing for two of the Home

26

Unions is not recorded. Suffice it to say that he is the only man who has ever played for two Unions in the International Championship.

RUGBY VERSUS SOCCER

LONDON, APRIL 1892

Imagine the British Lions taking on the cream of the country's soccer players at a selection of different sports. Jeremy Guscott sprinting 100 metres against Michael Owen perhaps, Scott Quinnell putting the shot against Paul Gascoigne, or Robert Howley contesting the high jump against David Beckham. And then soccer and rugby games between the teams, before rounding off the event with a limited-overs cricket match involving elevens skippered by Martin Johnson and Alan Shearer.

Far-fetched? Maybe. Yet in 1892 precisely such an unusual sporting challenge featuring the nation's leading footballers and rugby players occurred in a charity festival at Queen's Club in West Kensington.

The protagonists in this pioneering version of Superstars were the Barbarians Rugby Club and the Corinthians Football Club, two sides with such impeccable pedigrees that they were national institutions.

Formed in 1882, the Corinthians were keen to uphold the standards of amateur soccer at a time when the social background of the country's leading footballers was changing. In an earlier incarnation as the Wanderers the team had comprised old boys of the soccer-playing public schools and had won the FA Cup five times. But a tenet of its new constitution prohibited entry to league or cup competition (a rule that was later relaxed). University men and ex-public schools players dominated the club and so gentlemanly were the players that when the Corinthians conceded a penalty their goalkeeper was

28

removed to offer opponents a free shot at goal.

The Barbarians Rugby Club was less exclusive. Founded by an inveterate rugby tourist named Percy Carpmael at an oyster supper in Bradford in 1890, their membership was, in the words of the club's motto: 'for gentlemen in all classes but no bad sportsmen in any class.'

The unique sporting challenge of 1892 was issued by the Corinthians, whose squad included nine players who were or who would become soccer internationals. There were eight established or future rugby caps in the Barbarians' ranks, so it would be fair to conclude that the two codes were pretty well represented when the festival began with an athletics competition followed by a football match on Boat Race Saturday, 9 April.

Despite winning four of the track events the Baa-Baas struggled in the field events, where the matchless talents of one C B Fry were displayed. Charles Fry was arguably the best all-round sportsman who ever lived. An athletics, cricket and soccer Blue at Oxford, he would have added a Rugby Blue but for a leg injury. He played soccer and cricket for England and even found time to set the world long jump record.

On this particular day, playing for the Corinthians, he won both the long jump and high jump comfortably to reduce a commanding Barbarians lead and the outcome of the athletics was decided in the Corinthians' favour on the final event, the mile.

Fry then excelled for the Corinthians in the soccer match where the famous Walters brothers, Arthur and Percy, who had played together as full-backs for the England XI, were unperturbed by the unusual tactics of the rugby men. The Barbarians amused the crowd by instinctively resorting to the hand-off as a device for parrying opponents. A hat-trick by Tom Lindley helped the Corinthians to an easy 6–0 win, and after the first day of competition the footballers were two up with two to play.

Surely the Barbarians would resume two days later with a win in the rugby contest? For that match their side would be reinforced by several members of the England pack that a month earlier had completed a Triple Crown of victories in the International Championship without conceding a single score.

But they lost. Displaying astonishing ingenuity the dribblers outwitted the handlers. Lindley again showed himself to be a skilful games player, crossing for two tries and impressing the rugby men with his prodigious punting in a 14–12 victory. Newspaper reports of the match suggested that the referee was not fully acquainted with rugby's off-side laws. Even so, the Barbarians were gracious in defeat and many years later one of their committee members recalled, 'the Corinthians were entitled to the glory that follows a fully substantiated challenge.'

The rugby players did salvage some respect when the sides met again late in April for the cricket match. Batting first, the Corinthians were dismissed for 170 with C B Fry, thinly disguised as 'A Fryer' on the scorecards, falling for only 25 runs. Australians would consider Fry's wicket cheap at twice that price in several Ashes Tests in later years.

The Barbarians went on to win by four wickets, thanks mainly to an unbeaten 55 from one John Le Fleming, a former England wing threequarter who was a more than useful performer in the Kent XI. Thus a charming sporting challenge unparalleled in the annals of Britain's two footballing codes ended 3–1 in favour of the soccer players.

WHEN THE CROWD DIDN'T KNOW THE SCORE

CARDIFF, JANUARY 1893

For sheer drama before, during and after a match, the Wales-England encounter of January 1893 took some beating. It was the tenth match of the series and the first that these two sides had played at Cardiff.

The London contingent of the England team travelled down from Paddington on the Friday eve of the match and were unsure whether the game would take place. The south of Britain had been gripped in the jaws of a severe frost for the best part of a month, and the temperature was still well below freezing with snow in the air as the steaming Great Western locomotive pulled into Cardiff station to deliver the England side and accompanying press party.

An eerie, orange hue illuminated the players' short path to their headquarters at the Angel Hotel and the air hung heavy with the smell of burning coal. On their way to the hotel the players passed the Arms Park ground, and one of the pressmen peering through the hoardings compared the sight to a scene from Dante's *Inferno*.

The explanation was that the pitch had become so hard during the prolonged cold spell that the Cardiff groundsman had engaged an army of helpers to keep fire devils (small portable braziers of the type used by street workmen) blazing through the night in an attempt to soften the frosty turf and make it playable for the big match. More than 18 tons of coal were used as workers toiled through the night to thaw the ground.

The plan succeeded, though hundreds of muddy black squares alternated with harder, icy patches to lend the pitch a bizarre chessboard appearance as the two teams emerged early the next afternoon.

Arthur 'Monkey' Gould, the Welsh captain, was the idol of the Welsh sporting public. The outstanding threequarter of his day, he was also a noted athlete who owed his nickname to his remarkable agility. A dark, handsome man of 28, he had led the Wales XV for four years and was the senior cap in the side. His colleagues had the utmost respect for the Newport man, who had seven of his black-and-amber clubmates with him in the Welsh team.

Andrew Stoddart, the dual international who skippered England at Test cricket and who in 1888 had led the first British rugby touring team to Australia and New Zealand, captained the England side. Winning the toss, he chose to make first use of a biting easterly wind.

The game developed into a titanic tussle between the Welsh backs and English forwards. For seven years before this game the Welsh national side had been committed to playing four threequarters, a Cardiff club innovation which had never gone down too well with the sizeable Newport contingent that regularly graced Welsh XVs of this time. England in 1893 still preferred to use the orthodox three threequarter system, and their nine forwards made good use of their one-man advantage to create a couple of tries in the early stages of the match.

At half-time the visitors had what seemed an unassailable seven point lead but, undaunted, Gould spoke optimistically with his men during the interval and gave them inspiration soon after the restart. A Welsh lineout deep inside their own half was the springboard for an exhilarating passing movement which culminated in a try by the captain. Next, a bout of passing by the Welsh threequarters made an overlap for wing Norman Biggs to dash over in the corner.

That second Welsh try was subsequently viewed as the ultimate vindication of the four threequarter system in international rugby. By January 1894, all four of the Home Unions had adopted the formation and never again were nine forwards seen at international level.

The success of the Welsh threequarters against England, however, was more remarkable for the fact that their left centre, Conway Rees, had been playing with a broken collar-bone and could only take and give his passes with one hand. Rees eventually had to withdraw in pain to the touchline and when England's Howard Marshall crossed for his third try (in his one and only Test appearance), Welsh hopes of pulling off a first home victory against England took a dive.

Gould again revived their ambitions with a try from a splendid solo effort that took his side to within a score of England. Then, in the dying moments of the game, Wales were awarded a penalty near the touchline on the England 25. Gould summoned Billy Bancroft, the confident little Swansea full-back, to take a place kick for goal.

An argument appeared to follow. Bancroft, knowing well the hazards associated with place-kicking on a soft and slippery surface, defied his captain and steadied himself (much to the displeasure of Gould) for a drop-kick. The crowd of 20,000 – a record for a Welsh international up to that time – gasped as it saw Gould take offence and turn his back on Bancroft. Undeterred, the full-back let fly with his drop towards the Taff end of the ground, and before the ball had reached the highest point of its trajectory Bancroft turned and shouted to his captain: 'It's there, Arthur.'

Bancroft had kicked the first penalty goal in international rugby and immediately the referee whistled for the end of the game. But what was the final score? Wales finished with a goal from a try, a penalty goal and two tries to England's goal from a try and three tries.

The majority of spectators left under the impression that the result was a 14-all draw, in line with the scoring values then in vogue in Welsh rugby. But in fact the International Board, the body that laid down the laws for the conduct of international matches, had met only two days before the match and ruled that all goals should be worth three points and tries two. There had been little publicity regarding the change but the mathematics of the matter added up to a 12–11 win for Wales, even though most supporters had left the ground unaware of their side's famous victory.

Wales went on to win the Triple Crown for the first time, penalty goals were to become the bane of international rugby and scoring values were to change several times in the following hundred years as the International Board sought to reward tries above penalty goals.

THE STRANGE DISMISSAL

SYDNEY, JULY 1893

The 1893 New Zealand touring team to Australia played two series of representative matches: one against Queensland and the other against New South Wales during an eleven-match tour. Their last match of the visit was the third and deciding match of the rubber with the New South Welshmen. The tourists had won the first game 17–8, but suffered their only defeat of the tour 25–3 in the second match of the series.

They wrapped up the tour in style with a convincing 16–0 victory but there was a curious incident in the second half. The referee, Edward McCausland, was a New Zealander who had settled in Sydney a few years earlier. He stopped play near the end to speak to the New Zealand forward, William McKenzie.

McKenzie was the first New Zealander to practise wing-forward tactics and his nefarious activities had earned him the nickname 'Offside Mac'. After a long conversation with the referee he was seen limping towards the touch-line where the 20,000 spectators, under the impression that he was retiring injured, with one accord gave him a warm round of applause.

Afterwards the wily McKenzie was rumbled. He hadn't been injured at all: he had actually been sent off and had tried to disguise the fact by feigning injury. He thus became the first man to receive his marching orders while playing for New Zealand.

EVERYONE SCORED

RIPON, OCTOBER 1893

Ripon Grammar School was in the news recently when there was an attempt by local people to overturn its policy on selection and effectively remove its long-held Grammar status.

But a much earlier appearance in the headlines was made when the school earned a place among the curiosities of rugby union football. In October 1893, in a game against Richmond Grammar School, the rugby team scored a massive total of 112 points. This score comprised a dozen converted tries, a dropped goal and 16 unconverted tries.

One member of the team crossed for ten of the tries while another grabbed four tries, dropped a goal and kicked eight of the conversions. The remaining 13 players managed to share the remainder of the points, so that every member of the fifteen contributed to the total.

PITCHED INTO THE CROWD

CARDIFF, MARCH 1899

Full-back Billy Bancroft was a legend in Welsh rugby during the last decade of the nineteenth century. He played in every Welsh international between 1890 and 1901, during which time it was his proud boast that he had taken every place-kick awarded to his country.

Bancroft was a dashing player who enjoyed making opponents look clumsy. He also had a reputation for one-upmanship, as the following tale told by a distinguished Welsh full-back of a later vintage, Viv Jenkins, reveals.

Jenkins, like Bancroft, had also been a Glamorgan cricketer and in 1950, when Bancroft was approaching 80, he took the great man to Lord's to watch Gilbert Parkhouse, the Glamorgan opening bat, play for England against the West Indies.

That summer, New Zealand were hosting a Lions tour and Bob Scott was enjoying a successful rugby series playing for the All Blacks. The former full-backs, during a lull in the cricket, turned their conversation to rugby and in particular to the kicking feats of Bob Scott, who was also a full-back. Jenkins remarked to Bancroft that Scott, apparently, could kick goals from the half-way-line and in his bare feet. Bancroft's reply was: 'Ask him if he can place a goal from the corner flag' . . . the implication being that he, Bancroft, was perfectly capable of that difficult feat in his playing days.

But, returning to Bancroft's era in the 1890s, hardly anything fazed him on a rugby pitch, though he did admit that he was once astonished by his Irish counterpart in an international at Llanelli early in his career. At Stradey Park in 1891 the Irish full-back, Dolway Walkington, who was very short-sighted, turned out wearing a monocle. (Quite what the Llanelli faithful made of that does not seem to have been recorded.) Even Bancroft, however, had to admire the man later in the game when Walkington caught a loose kick ahead, calmly removed his eye-piece and dropped a goal.

There was one occasion, though, also against Ireland, where opponents really did get the better of the Welsh full-back. In March 1899, Ireland came to Cardiff in search of the Triple Crown. They had never beaten Wales there and a record crowd overflowed onto the pitch before the match started. Although the teams marched out on time for the start of the match, the kick-off had to be delayed for thirty minutes or so while the police and officials persuaded the crowd to move back from the field of play.

Once the game commenced, spectators regularly encroached on to the field of play and one observer noted that at times Wales appeared to have the help of 'a thousand full-backs'. The match was tight and the heavy Irish forwards gave a much-vaunted Welsh pack a torrid time. Ireland won through the only try of the match, scored in the first half.

Then the unruly crowd again spilled on to the field of play at the interval and Mr Adam Turnbull, the Scottish referee, spent the best part of a quarter of an hour begging spectators to retreat.

Soon after the match restarted Bancroft made a teasing run across the field towards the touchline. It was a favourite ruse of his to give opposing forwards the run around and so tire them. On this occasion he did not bargain for the consequences of his actions. For once, he was caught by two of the biggest forwards then playing international rugby. The Ryan brothers, Mick and Jack from Tipperary, were noted track and field athletes who had also played Gaelic Football, but as rugby forwards they were classified as having more brawn than brain. Yet they managed to catch Bancroft and dumped him unceremoniously over the touchline . . . where he landed awkwardly among the densely packed crowd.

Bancroft sustained painful injuries, including a couple of fractured ribs, and for the only time in his 33 successive Welsh appearances had to finish a match prematurely.

OXFORD WIN WITH 14 MEN

LONDON, DECEMBER 1900

In the days before substitutes were permitted, the incidence of big matches won by teams depleted through injury was rare. True, Ireland overturned a 0–6 deficit to come back and beat a strong Welsh team in 1904 when they had only 14 fit men on the field for most of the second half. But the game that the old-timers always referred to when discussing results where one team splendidly overcame the odds was the 1900 Varsity match.

The annual battle of the Blues was traditionally held at the Queen's Club in West Kensington at this time. In the lead-up to the match both Universities had compiled similar records so that on the day of the game the betting was described as 'even money'. It was felt that Cambridge had the stronger forwards, while Oxford possessed the more creative back division.

Oxford suffered a cruel blow early in the match when one of their wings, John Crawfurd, who was an Irish trialist, injured his right shoulder so severely in a tackle that he had to leave the field and played no further part in the game. At first, Oxford refused to withdraw a man from their pack, preferring to risk leaving a position uncovered behind the scrum. With great relief, thanks to some rib-jarring tackling by Jack Crabbie, Oxford reached half-time without having conceded a score.

In the second half, superior Cambridge scrummaging began to take its effect and, helped by two tries scored by their wing, Alfred Hind, they built an 8–0 lead. At this stage, Oxford finally conceded a forward from the pack to cover the gap in the threequarter line. There followed an amazing swing in the fortunes of the match.

'To have the odds against you [in the Varsity match] is the most inspiring challenge of all,' wrote Howard Marshall of this match many years later when recalling Oxford's rearguard action. First, a well backed up sweeping move took play fully sixty yards before Ernest Walton raced over for 'one of the finest [tries] in the history of the [Varsity] match'. The try was converted, leaving Cambridge only three points clear.

'This infused fresh life on the contest,' revealed the *Daily Telegraph*, 'and clearly had a disconcerting influence upon the Cambridge men.' Seven minutes from the end, Frank Jones of Cambridge was slow to recover a loose ball and Crabbie was quickly up to sprint away for a try at the posts. The conversion put Oxford 10–8 ahead.

'Even the most phlegmatic spectator could hardly bear to watch,' continued Marshall, until 'after minutes which seemed like hours Mr Harnett's whistle for no-side left Oxford magnificently victorious.' The *Telegraph* concluded: 'Altogether it was a great game, one of the best played between the two Universities.'

UNIQUE HAT TRICK

SWANSEA, JANUARY 1903

Even today tries by tight forwards are rare. Hat tricks of tries scored by such forwards are virtually unknown. But nearly one hundred years ago a Welsh forward performed this remarkable feat in an international match against England at Swansea. It will come as no surprise to learn that the record he set that day has never been matched in an International Championship match. Admittedly, the player who scored that unique hat trick did have an advantage – he played as an emergency wing.

Conditions at St Helen's in Swansea were awful. It was a typical west Wales day with a heavy grey sky bringing slanting rain in from the Mumbles. The band that performed before the teams ran on to the pitch even had to stop playing momentarily when their instruments filled with water.

The Welsh captain and left wing was Tom Pearson, who scored a tenth-minute try to give Wales the lead. But five minutes later the captain was injured when he fell clumsily after a tackle by the English full-back. Pearson was forced to retire and the young Newport forward, Jehoida Hodges, was withdrawn from the Welsh pack and posted to the left-wing.

The Welsh forwards showed no signs of missing their colleague. Shortly after Pearson had retired, they heeled to their half-backs and fly-half Llewellyn Lloyd made a neat break to send his partner, Dickie Owen, in for a try.

Then, in an astonishing twenty minutes leading up to the interval, Hodges ran in a genuine hat trick of tries: three in a row. The ball passed through several pairs of hands before the

Welsh centres worked him clear on the left to run in for his first try. Next, Rees Gabe capitalised on poor handling by his opponent to send Hodges over for a second and, shortly before half-time, Strand Jones, the Welsh full-back, initiated a move from half-way that culminated in the Newport forward's third try. At the break Wales led 21–0 and were home and dry.

The critics were quick to point out that the kudos for the Welsh win was with their seven-man pack and the smooth-working efficiency of their handling. Hodges, it was added, had only to take the ball and score on each occasion. Still, the fact that he took his passes and had the positional sense to be in the right place at the right time is ample testimony to the skills and intelligence of a player who was better known for his strength at the scrummages and effectiveness in the line-outs.

Two prop forwards of the modern era went on to match Hodges's feat in friendly internationals. In 1964, when the Fijians made their first tour of Europe, they wound up their successful visit with an unofficial international against Wales at Cardiff Arms Park.

On a glorious sunny day in late September, the Fijians appealed to the hearts of a sell-out Welsh crowd by running the then Five Nations champions to an exciting 28–22 scoreline. The most extraordinary point about the match was that the Fijian prop, Sevaro Walisoliso, ran in a hat-trick of tries.

The only other prop who scored three tries in a cap match was Christian Califano, the versatile Toulouse and France front-ranker, who is in so many ways the perfect embodiment of the modern tight forward. Showing a surprising turn of speed, agility of thought and sleight of hand he crossed for his hat-trick against Romania in Aurillac in 1996.

A FAMILY AFFAIR

GREYTOWN, JULY 1903

Irish rugby has been noted down the years for the considerable number of brotherly pairs and even trios who have represented the country. The record, however, for most brothers appearing together in a first-class team was first established by the Smiths of Bush in New Zealand.

Five of them took the field for the visiting Bush side in a unique family affair against Wairarapa at Greytown in July 1903. They were full-back George, centre Bill and forwards Gordon, Bob and Campbell. For the record, the quintet were in a 0–16 losing side and never again played together.

They are not well remembered now, even in New Zealand. But conversely, the brothers who equalled the record 58 years later belonged to one of the most famous of all New Zealand rugby-playing clans and are unlikely to be forgotten.

In 1961, the Clarkes of Waikato provided the province with Don (full-back), Doug (centre), Ian (prop), Graeme and Brian (both second-row locks) for the 11–8 win against Thames Valley at Te Aroha. Don and Ian were established All Blacks who, between them, appeared in 55 Tests for New Zealand.

A UNIQUE SCOTTISH TREBLE

JOHANNESBURG, AUGUST 1903

The opening Test of the 1903 British/Irish tour of South Africa at the Wanderers ground provided a unique line-up of captains and referee. The trio were all Scottish internationals. The South African captain was a former Scotland cap, the referee was also an ex-Scotland international, and the leader of the British team was the current Scotland rugby captain.

The tourists' captain, Mark Morrison, was a Scottish farmer who had been first capped as a teenager in 1896. He was still a relative youngster when he took over the leadership of the Scotland side in 1899, and he held the post through 15 internationals up to 1904, to establish a Scottish record that stood unbeaten for more than 70 years. He led Scotland to Triple Crowns in 1901 and 1903.

His opposite number as captain in the South African pack was Alex Frew who, two years earlier, had played under Morrison in the Triple Crown side. Frew was a native of Kilmarnock who qualified as a doctor from Edinburgh University before emigrating to the Transvaal as a young man. Playing alongside him in the Test was another former Scotland forward, Saxon McEwan, who had won 16 caps between 1894 and 1900 and, like Frew, had sought fame and fortune in the Transvaal.

Bill Donaldson, the referee, completed the unique Scottish treble. Donaldson was a former pupil of Loretto School who won Oxford Blues in 1892–4 and later became an iron merchant. A half-back who was one of the first to appreciate the value of tactical kicking, he played six times for Scotland in the 1890s and, in his last international, against Ireland in 1899, he had the distinction of becoming the first Scotsman to score on Scotland's new national ground (at Inverleith, Edinburgh) when he kicked his team's sole penalty goal.

The Test in South Africa appropriately ended in a 10–10 draw, with Alex Frew leading the South Africans by example and scoring one of their two tries. The second Test finished in a scoreless draw, before South Africa took the series with victory in the third. It was the first time that South Africa had won a Test series. They would not lose one at home for another 55 years.

PRIMITIVE TRAVEL ARRANGEMENTS

CORK, FEBRUARY 1905

Modern travel arrangements and the five-star accommodation enjoyed by first-class players today are a far cry from the journey of 1905, when England travelled to Cork to play Ireland in an international at the Mardyke Road ground.

After making a long and uncomfortable boat crossing to Dun Laoghaire, the England team had to endure a gruelling train journey from Dublin across the country to Cork, in which they were 'packed like sardines into a third-class smoker', according to the late E H D Sewell, who was among the press party attending the game. 'Anyone familiar with train journeys in Ireland [in those days] will tell you what that preparation for a match must have been like,' he added.

England were obviously affected by the travelling conditions and Ireland won by the handsome margin of 17–3. To add insult to England's injuries, Basil Maclear, who scored one of Ireland's tries, was a Portsmouth-born Bedford player who had been judged 'not good enough' to play for England by the Rugby Football Union's selectors.

DISBELIEVING SPORTS EDITORS

EXETER, SEPTEMBER 1905

They came, they played, and they almost completely conquered. The original New Zealand All Blacks, the first fully representative overseas Dominion side to undertake a Test tour of Europe, played 33 matches in Britain, Ireland and France in the first half of the 1905–6 season, winning 32 and losing only once.

The tour party arrived in England on 8 September, and made its headquarters at Newton Abbot, where the visitors prepared for their first match of the tour against Devon at Exeter. The only foreknowledge the English press and players had of New Zealand methods was from players who had visited the land of the long black cloud with Darkie Bedell-Sivright's British team twelve months earlier. Although New Zealand (9–3) and Auckland (13–0) had defeated the British side then, few among the London press corps expected the men in black to succeed on a long, arduous tour in British conditions.

Opinion expressed in the leading British newspapers in the lead-up to the Devon match was that at best the New Zealanders would emerge with honours even. The county were the champions of the South-West (and, indeed, went on to win the English county championship the same season). Views, however, would have to be altered within ten minutes of the kick-off. The tourists simply ran riot. After three minutes James Hunter broke the Devon defence for the first try of the tour. Billy Wallace, who played throughout the match in a sun-hat, converted and then added a penalty. From there on, in the

48

words of the New Zealand manager, George Dixon, 'scores came thick and fast'.

By half-time it was 27–0 and the full-time score was a staggering 55–4. Reporters at the game transmitted the result through to their newspapers ahead of filing their full match reports. When the numbers came in to the various offices preparing their early editions of the Sunday papers, many sports editors were surprised by the score. As winning totals of 50 points were virtually unknown in senior matches at that time, several editors felt there must have been a transmission error and took it upon themselves to 'correct' the scores. One newspaper changed the score to read New Zealand 5, Devon 4 whilst another, acknowledging the strength of Devon rugby, ran with the headline Devon 55, New Zealand 4.

A month later, no such doubts would be expressed. By mid-October the All Blacks had won the first eleven matches of their visit, piling up 408 points and conceding only seven – including just one try. British rugby was beginning to learn its place in the game's global order.

THE REFEREE PERFORMS A SOLO

RICHMOND, NOVEMBER 1905

By the end of October, the All Blacks had played and won 13 matches on the English leg of their tour. Their game with Surrey on the first day of November was remarkable on two counts: for the first time their winning margin was less than a dozen points and the referee was the star of the match.

He awarded 14 penalties against the New Zealanders in the first half alone, and whistled continuously for a procession of minor offences that at first amused but later irritated the crowd. Mr Dixon, the tourists' diplomatic manager, noted: 'From the first, penalty kicks were given with great frequency against New Zealand, generally for infringements in the scrum which, from my position in the stand, were not discoverable.'

More than 10,000 had turned up to see the tourists, about whom the chattering classes were all talking, make only their second appearance in the capital. The referee, it was reported, 'was evidently under the impression that everybody had come to hear him perform on the whistle'.

The *Daily Mail*'s critic went to town. Under the banner headline, 'Whistling Fantasia by the Referee,' he proceeded to send up the official at every opportunity. Thus a lady spectator is reported as asking her escort: 'Why aren't the New Zealanders allowed to have a man whistle for them, too?' And when the All Blacks eventually opened the scoring after 25 minutes, with half-back Fred Roberts darting over from a scrum, the report continued, 'When the referee showed signs of fatigue the tourists seized the opportunity to score. The

50

explanation advanced for the referee's lapse was that the pea in his whistle had stuck'.

The pea must have lodged twice more in the second half as New Zealand added two more tries to win 11–0, easily their narrowest margin of victory throughout the English part of the tour. The long-suffering crowd went away whistling and 'instead of the usual rush for the jerseys of the scorers, the crowd made a wild scramble for the referee's whistle at the end'.

The name of this virtuoso? None other than Mr Williams of the Rugby Football Union's committee, the genius who a couple of years later identified for the Union the potential of the market garden site at Twickenham that became known as Billy Williams's Cabbage Patch. Williams was a well-known international referee at this time but, significantly, was not called on to officiate at any of the All Blacks' remaining 20 matches in Europe after his Richmond débâcle.

GALLANT LITTLE WALES

CARDIFF, DECEMBER 1905

Arguably the game's most famous controversy was spawned in December 1905. The All Blacks' invincible playing record was on the line when they ventured into Wales for the first time on their tour. The Welsh were the reigning European champions and holders of the Triple Crown, and the showdown with the New Zealanders was greatly anticipated.

Hundreds of rugby enthusiasts packed the platform at Newport station to catch a glimpse of the tourists as the train carrying them to Wales made its first stop in the Principality. Less than a half-hour later they were enjoying a magnificent reception at Cardiff General from, according to New Zealand manager, George Dixon, 'the largest crowd that met us on tour'.

The Saturday of the match, though cold and grey, was dry and still and more than 40,000 crammed the old wooden stands and enclosures of the Arms Park. The gates were shut long before the kick-off and when the sides entered the playing enclosure they were given an enthusiastic welcome. The New Zealanders performed their traditional haka. The Welsh players, in response, engaged the choral legions in a moving rendition of 'Land of my fathers'. The singing charged the electric atmosphere and clearly had an effect on the visitors. 'It was a wonderful sight,' Mr Dixon noted in his diary.

Wales had the better of the first half-hour's play. Their forwards were prominent in the loose and packed tightly against their much-vaunted opponents in the scrums. It came as no surprise, therefore, when they opened the scoring about nine minutes before half-time.

Dickie Owen gathered the ball at a scrum on the All Blacks' 25 and feinted to give an orthodox scrum-half pass to his partner, Percy Bush. Now Bush had toured New Zealand with the British team some 18 months earlier and as a result of his escapades on that visit commanded huge respect from the tourists. The New Zealand defence were anxious to bottle up this Welsh genie so, sensing that he was about to gain possession, they swung towards the open-side where Bush was lining up an attack.

Seeing that the defence was committed to Bush, Owen threw a perfectly-judged reverse pass to the narrow side, where Cliff Pritchard and Rees Gabe completed a well-rehearsed move to work an overlap for Teddy Morgan to race along the left wing and score in the corner. Bert Winfield failed to convert and Wales went into the interval nursing a slender 3–0 lead.

The tale of the second half is easily told: time after time New Zealand attacked; time after time Wales repulsed them with long, raking relieving punts to touch or hard, effective tackles. Near the end, however, came the incident that overshadowed the match. From a run out of defence Billy Wallace made more than 30 yards before passing on to his centre, Bob Deans, who went full-pelt for the line. Many thought that he had crossed for a try but the referee, John Dallas of Scotland, ruled that Deans had been held up in a tackle and rejected claims for a score. Even on his death-bed, it was claimed, Mr Dallas reiterated that Deans did not score.

The *Daily Mail*, which gave the match three full columns of broadsheet coverage, sparked off the controversy which has now lasted nearly a century. 'Defeated By Gallant Little Wales,' ran its headline, but the telling paragraph that appeared near the end of the match report was as follows: '[Deans] was collared but not before he had crossed the Welsh line, though the referee, whose decision is bound to be accepted in such matters, declared that he had been held up and ordered a scrum instead of a place kick [at goal].'

'Those in the best position to judge,' it continued, 'state that Deans grounded the ball six inches over the line, and some of the Welsh players admit that the equalising try was actually scored, and that Deans, after crossing the line, was pulled back.' New Zealanders have never forgotten the story and, to this day, the first port of call of many Kiwis visiting Cardiff is to the Arms Park to see the spot where Deans didn't score.

THE CHIEF CONSTABLE SAVES WALES

CARDIFF, FEBRUARY 1906

Matches between Wales and Scotland invariably settled the International Championship title in the first decade of the twentieth century. A look at the roll of honour for those years will show the reader that the nations exercised a duopoly over international rugby, either Wales or Scotland finishing top of the table every year from 1900 to 1909.

Wales were reigning champions and recent victors over the All Blacks when the nations met for their annual bash in front of 25,000 at Cardiff in 1906. Scotland had been beaten 12–7 by the New Zealanders in a closely contested match but entered the Welsh game full of optimism.

High social status was attached to attendance at Wales's matches at the turn of the century, and even the Chief Constable of Cardiff felt that he should be seen to be on active duty when international rugby matches were played on his patch. On this particular occasion he turned out in his finery as usual, though little did he realise that he was about to play a part in the evolution of the game's laws.

Early in the match, Scotland were pressing. 'Darky' Bedell-Sivright, a former Lions captain and a strapping wing forward who was renowned for his dribbling powers, led a Scottish rush into the Welsh 25 and a try seemed certain. He toed the ball over the Welsh line but was astonished to see it strike 'the might and majesty of the stalwart Chief Constable' who at that moment was strutting his stuff up and down the Welsh in-goal area.

The Scot reacted quickly, changed direction and managed to touch the ball down to claim a try. But Mr Allen, the Irish referee, ruled 'dead ball' and Scotland's chance of taking the lead was lost. Later in the half, Wales scored tries through Jehoida Hodges and Cliff Pritchard, two of the heroes of their victory over the All Blacks, and finished the match winners by 9–3. Wales went on to retain the International Championship.

But the good Chief Constable later warranted his own footnote to the history of the game's laws. The International Board, the body that frames rugby's rules and regulations, subsequently reflected long and hard on the events at Cardiff and introduced a new clause to ensure that any repeat act should be fairly covered.

The outcome of their deliberations was to rule that in future referees should regard all officials and spectators as offending players on the home side, and that any doubt regarding a point or score arising should be awarded against the side responsible for the ground arrangements.

SELECTORS' COCK-UP

LONDON, DECEMBER 1906

One can accept that in the early days of international rugby travelling problems or communication difficulties contributed to teams arriving one or perhaps two short for a big match. But surely the mix-up surrounding the selection of the 1906 England team to face the First Springboks was inexcusable.

One of the prominent forwards of the early part of the 1906–7 season was a Liverpool and Lancashire player named Noel Slocock, who was making a reputation as an effective line-out jumper. The main England trial in those days was the North-South match, and he had already given a tidy account of himself in one of those encounters when the England selectors sat down to deliberate over the XV to meet South Africa at the Crystal Palace in December 1906.

Slocock's name was, by all accounts, put forward for the match but when the team was announced his name was omitted owing to a clerical error. Instead, the name of Arnold Alcock appeared in the team lists. Alcock was a medical student at Guy's Hospital and no more than a useful forward in their Hospitals' Cup side. Yet he was to gain his cap at Slocock's expense.

The student doctor played a part in a creditable 3–3 draw but reports of the match do not single him out for praise. He was never invited to take part in a trial and never again played for England. In later life, however, he was the shining example of the past player who puts something back into the game.

He settled in general practice in Gloucester and from 1924

until 1969 served the club as president. He died in 1973, aged 91, and was the last survivor of his one and only England XV.

Noel Slocock scored a try for the Lancashire XV that made the South Africans work hard for victory in their first match after the England Test and, tellingly, came into the England team for their next international. He became a regular member of their pack for two seasons until his playing career ended in 1908, after captaining a losing England side in the Calcutta Cup match. He died young, killed in action in France in 1916.

DEFEAT IN THE FOG

BRISTOL, JANUARY 1908

Mercifully few rugby matches have been badly affected by fog down the years. In recent times the only game that was completely ruined as a spectacle by dense fog was between the touring Australian schoolboys and England 19 group at Twickenham in January 1978.

Though schoolboys, the tourists had won widespread acclaim for their attacking ploys on that tour. Forwards and backs were supremely fit and, with the instinctive genius of the three Ella brothers behind the scrum, the Australians arrived at Twickenham for their showdown against England with 13 wins in 13 games to their name.

A large crowd made the journey to Twickenham with the keenest anticipation, only to catch glimpses of the game as play approached the touchlines or corners. The Twickenham authorities were enlightened enough to permit spectators to wander close to the goal lines and dead-ball-lines in order to secure a clearer view of the proceedings. So thick was the fog that play itself was threatened. Only the fluid, intelligent refereeing of France's Jean-Pierre Bonnet ensured that at least the players enjoyed the afternoon. The Australians especially: they scored seven tries, missed all their conversion kicks (couldn't see the posts in all probability) and won handsomely by 31–9.

The only major international badly affected by fog was the 1908 England-Wales game. As the Rugby Football Union were making plans for the development of Twickenham at the time, international matches were taken to fresh venues around the country. This match was scheduled for the Bristol City AFC ground and more than 25,000 of the Bristol faithful turned up to sit in eerie silence as occasionally a player emerged from the mist.

'At no time was it possible to see distinctly the width of the field of play, and in the later stages the occupants of the stands frequently lost sight of both teams,' the *Daily Telegraph* related. 'It was a singular match, played amid exasperating surroundings.'

One of the players who took part in that game was Rees Gabe, the Llanelli, Cardiff and Wales centre who in later years was a respected rugby critic. Recalling the Bristol fog match he was later to give some interesting insights: 'In the second half no spectators could be seen from the centre of the field. The scoring was phenomenal, because we had to rely more on our ears than our eyes to discover where the ball was bouncing.'

Wales won 28–18 with Percy Bush, their cheeky fly-half, setting the ball rolling with a dropped goal in the opening minutes of the match. Bush was an artful dodger at the best of times. Playing against him in the fog must have been doubly difficult, and in reporting the many strange incidents that occurred during the course of the game there can be no doubt that the tricky Bush was at the centre of Welsh moves to confound the English defence. He later scored a try and, so it was told, had a hand in three others scored by Wales. England for the most part were left chasing ghosts.

The story runs that after the match the Welsh side were relaxing in their tubs when it was realised that full-back Bert Winfied was missing. One of the Welsh officials went back out to the pitch, called his name and discovered that the Cardiff player was still out there peering through the fog, thinking his team were maintaining an attacking position.

Arguably the worst effect fog had on a big match was in 1890–1, causing three postponements of the Varsity match. The games were staged in Kensington until 1921, when Twickenham became home to the annual match.

The original 1890 fixture was fixed for 10 December but a London pea-souper obscured the ground. Both sides had travelled to Queen's Club for the fixture but no play took place and the match was re-arranged for 18 February. Fog again caused a postponement, and a third cancellation was necessary a week later when West Kensington was again shrouded in mist and the teams were cabled advising them not to make the journey to London.

The match was eventually played at the fourth attempt on 2 March and resulted in a draw.

SEVEN BROTHERS VERSUS SEVEN BROTHERS

CARMARTHEN, APRIL 1909

The credit for devising the seven-a-side version of rugby goes to Ned Haig, a local butcher who arranged the first tournament in Melrose at the end of the 1882–3 season. Within two years there were annual sevens competitions staged at Gala and Hawick and by the turn of the century the abbreviated game had established a unique end-of-season circuit in the Scottish Borders.

Special permission had to be obtained from the Rugby Unions to allow such tournaments to take place and it was not until the 1920s that sevens became a feature of the season in England. Tournaments were long outlawed because they led to the award of prize money, in direct contravention of the laws pertaining to amateurism.

One of the most unusual sevens challenges took place in West Wales at Easter 1909, when a family of seven Williams brothers from Haverfordwest in Pembrokeshire took on the seven Randall brothers of Llanelli. The match was staged on neutral ground at Carmarthen, roughly halfway between the two towns, where more than a thousand of the brothers' travelling supporters turned up to see the 'Family Champion-ship of the United Kingdom'. There was a £100 prize at stake and both sides employed their own trainers to assist with their preparations for a match that was refereed by the ex-Welsh international full-back, Billy Bancroft of Swansea.

The Randalls were brawny steel workers and millmen typical

62

of the working population of Llanelli at the turn of the century. The Haverfordwest boys were sons of the local police superintendent, though none followed their father into the Constabulary. Three were hairdressers, three worked as commission agents and the seventh brother was a clerk.

The match itself was a scrappy, ill-tempered affair according to several local press reports. The Williamses lost one of their brothers through injury early on and Mr Bancroft had to intervene several times as the contest frequently threatened to degenerate into a glorified fight. 'It was more like a wrestling match,' Bancroft commented after the Williamses ran out 8–0 winners.

JOE'S NEW YEAR CAP

SWANSEA, JANUARY 1910

The first ever Five Nations match took place in January 1910 at Swansea, though it is doubtful whether the players who played in the game realised at the time that they were creating a piece of history, by launching what became the jewel in the northern hemisphere's rugby crown. The Five Nations tournament became the byword for European rugby at its best for the rest of the twentieth century.

But back in 1910, the competition came about by accident. France had entered the lists of international rugby on New Year's Day, 1906, with an international against the All Blacks. Later the same year, England crossed the Channel for their first taste of French rugby and two years later Wales hosted the newcomers for the first time. Ireland gave the French an inaugural fixture in 1909 before, the following year, Scotland decided that they, too, would join the *entente cordiale*.

So 1910 is the date from which Five Nations history is reckoned, simply because it was the first time that the round-robin of ten matches involving the nations was completed. The phrase *Tournoi des Cinq Nations* was coined by the French press as early as the 1920s, though its use in the Home Unions did not really catch on until the 1960s.

Could France have made a more inauspicious start to the competition than the events surrounding the departure of their team from Paris for their journey to Wales on New Year's Eve, 1909?

When the players and officials assembled to make their

journey to Swansea they discovered that one of their number, a new cap in the forwards named Hélier Tilh, had been forced to withdraw owing to military duties in Bordeaux. The boat train departed with 14 players aboard, leaving one of the French selectors to search the streets of the capital for someone to make up the pack.

At length, the weary official discovered one Joe Anduran working in a picture gallery on the Rue La Boétie. Anduran thought he was the butt of a practical joke when he was first approached about representing his country. Eventually he was persuaded that his services were genuinely required and he enthusiastically joined the selector in a taxi to gather his kit from home.

Preparations for New Year celebrations were well under way back at the Anduran household and poor Joe had plenty of explaining to do to his wife to excuse himself from the forth-coming family festivities. Nevertheless, despite his wife's displeasure, he set off for Swansea and eventually caught up with the rest of the French team on the morning of the match.

France were overwhelmed 49–14. The Welsh ran rings around their hapless visitors and raced over for ten tries to two in reply. Poor old Joe didn't even warrant a mention in any of the press reports of the match and he never again received an invitation to represent his country.

Even so, Mme Anduran must have forgiven him for his commitment to the game: in 1913, aged nearly 31, Joe turned out for his club, SCUF (a university sports club in Paris), in the final of the French Championship and collected a loser's medal in a side beaten by Bayonne.

The man who played rugby for his country at the drop of a hat in 1910 was just as quick to serve his country in more serious battles four years later. Joe joined the infantry at the outbreak of the Great War and survived barely two months before losing his life in the fighting south-east of Lens in October 1914. He was 32.

RIOTOUS ASSEMBLY

PARIS, JANUARY 1913

Several of the early international matches staged in Paris were noted for unruly behaviour among the home crowd. Visiting British journalists often ascribed this tendency to a lack of understanding by the French of the game's complex Laws.

Even as late as 1952, incidentally, when France played South Africa at Colombes, the French Federation, anxious to educate spectators, used to print the Laws of the Game on the back of match tickets. Parisians, they realised, were less well immersed in rugby's rules than followers from the south of the country where the game was almost a passion.

One of the worst crowd demonstrations that occurred before the Great War was on New Year's Day, 1913, when Scotland visited the old Parc des Princes to launch that season's Five Nations Championship.

More than 25,000 spectators paid more than 40,000 old French francs to see the Scots win by the comfortable margin of 21–3. Scotland had lost on their only previous visit to Paris and no doubt the big crowd had turned up in anticipation of witnessing another French success.

On the day, though, the strict refereeing interpretations of England's Mr Baxter riled the crowd. Baxter unstintingly applied the letter of the law, usually to France's cost. Scotland scored five tries to one and before the end of the game the partisan crowd wanted blood. It looked as if it would be Mr Baxter's when a faction in the crowd angrily closed in on him as he left the pitch at the end of the match. French officials and players moved quickly to protect him as demonstrating spectators threatened to riot. Not even the presence of mounted police quelled the crowd's antics.

In the end, the quick-thinking of France's wing, Pierre Failliot, saved the day. A former Olympic decathlete and holder of the French 400 metres record, he came to Baxter's rescue and escorted him at speed to safety behind the stands where a waiting taxi whisked the Englishman off to central Paris.

There was a sad sequel to this match. The Scottish Rugby Union were so disgusted by the reactions of the crowd that they immediately cancelled future fixtures with the French. No match took place between the nations the following season and it was not until 1920 that the series of Scotland-France matches was resumed.

Charles Usher, Scotland's captain in this match, told an amusing story about it in later years. Scotland's full-back in 1913 was Walter Dickson, a South African Rhodes scholar who was deaf. As the Scots walked off among the animated French crowd at the end of the game, Dickson completely misinterpreted the situation and said to his captain: 'It's awfully sporting of them to take their licking like this, isn't it?'

A DAY AT THE RACES

CORK, MARCH 1913

Many rugby players and former internationals enjoy the odd flutter on the horses. Several have become successful owners. John Douglas, the Scotland number eight who won a dozen caps in the early 1960s, arguably achieved the greatest distinction in this respect when his horse, Rubstic, won the 1979 Grand National. No doubt several of his former Scotland colleagues benefited that afternoon from a little bit of inside knowledge.

In earlier years, John Ryan, the strapping Irish forward who, with his brother Mick, helped Ireland carry off the Triple Crown in 1899, was a big follower of form and later went on to become a successful race-horse breeder. He, too, enjoyed an hour of glory at Aintree. In 1928, his Tipperary Tim came in at 100–1, one of the few rank outsiders ever to win the National.

And back in March 1964, on a wet and miserable day, those with an interest in the two sports had their work cut out to follow the big race on a day that coincided with two major rugby internationals – Wales v France and Scotland v England – upon which depended the outcome of that year's Five Nations Championship title. In the end Wales drew and Scotland won, leaving these two nations sharing the title, while the appropriately named Team Spirit triumphed at 18–1 in the Grand National.

Down the years, though, it is the Irish who have earned a reputation for enjoying their horse racing as much as their rugby football. The ideal holiday for an Irish sports lover is to cross the channel for Cheltenham week and take in an Ireland rugby international at Twickenham or Cardiff at the weekend.

This love of both sports has never been so admirably demonstrated as on 24 March, 1913 in Cork. The sporting calendar had placed the Ireland v France game on the same afternoon as the Cork races. This proved unacceptable to the Irish and, in order to allow both supporters and players to enjoy the Cork races as well as the rugby match, the game was staged in the morning – the only instance that an international match has kicked off so early for the sole purpose of accommodating another sporting event.

More than 8000 turned up to see Ireland trounce France 24–0 at the Wellington Bridge Ground on the Mardyke before turning their attention to the horses. A young Irish medical student, Joe Quinn, ran in a hat-trick of tries as Ireland stacked up what remains their record winning margin over the French. And after the game the players were transported to the race-course, where they were treated to a champagne lunch by the course executive.

A GAME OF FOUR QUARTERS

WELLINGTON, SEPTEMBER 1913

The weather in windy Wellington, New Zealand, has often led to unusual matches at the city's famous Athletic Park ground. One of the earliest Test matches affected by atrocious conditions was against the touring Wallabies of 1913. The match was the opening Test of a late-season series and was played in a continuous downpour. To make matters worse, a gale force wind caused the wind chill factor to drop below the freezing mark. One newspaper extolled the 5000 spectators who 'huddling together for warmth and protection from the elements [were] a patient and enduring umbrella and overcoat brigade.'

The referee for the match was Len Simpson, a warehouseman and local official who was in charge of his first Test. Mr Simpson, recognising that the conditions were likely to play a significant part in the run of play, hit on the novel idea of dividing the Test match into four equal periods of 20 minutes, with the sides swapping ends after each break. The players were revived with hot broth during the intervals, with some jumping at the chance to change into dry kit.

The weather became progressively worse as the game wore on and the poor, bedraggled Australians, very much at sea in such foreign conditions, fell further and further behind. New Zealand added three tries in the third and fourth quarters to finish 30–5 winners despite losing their first-choice half-back Henry Taylor, who was replaced at half-time by Frank Mitchinson, a threequarter.

Len Simpson was a front-line New Zealand referee for a decade and actually accompanied the 1924–5 All Blacks to Britain, Ireland and France as their touch-judge. But his unusual move to break a Test match into more than the customary two periods of play is, as far as can be ascertained, unique at international level.

WHERE'S MY SHIRT?

PARIS, JANUARY 1920

The Scottish Rugby Union had a reputation for conservatism and parsimony in the early years of international rugby. They were ardent upholders of the principles of amateurism and refused to meet Wales in 1898 and 1899, alleging that the Welsh Union were supporting professionalism by condoning the launch of a testimonial fund to Arthur Gould, the Welsh captain.

The Scots also harboured other reservations. They had doubts about playing international matches against touring sides and refused to meet the First Wallabies of 1908–9. Therefore, in the 1920s, when the numbering of players was almost universal in international matches, it was no surprise that the Scots were the last to conform. When King George V enquired of the Scottish president at Twickenham in 1924 as to why Scotland were not numbered, back came the reply to HM: 'This is a rugby match, not a cattle market.'

One of the most amusing stories relating to the Scottish Union's tightness was told by Jock Wemyss, who played rugby as a prop forward for Scotland before and after the Great War.

Scotland's first international after the Armistice was on New Year's Day 1920 in Paris, on the ground where the riot match of 1913 had been staged. In those days, players brought their own shorts and club socks to international matches, expecting only to receive their jerseys.

Sitting in the changing room at the Parc des Princes before the match, Wemyss was waiting for his jersey, but otherwise was ready to run out, when one of the Scottish selectors came in to distribute the navy blue shirts complete with thistle emblem. The selector bypassed Wemyss but carried on giving out the jerseys until none was left. At that point, Wemyss enquired about his shirt.

Turning to him, the selector said, 'You played before the war. You were supposed to bring your old shirt.' Despite remonstrating with the baggage man, Wemyss could not convince him that he had no shirt. Even the explanation that he had swapped his jersey with an opponent after his last match (six years earlier) would not wash.

It was only when Wemyss took his place bare-chested in the queue to file out on to the pitch that the Union's official eventually gave in and managed to rustle up a shirt for Jock to wear. Scotland won a hard game played in wet, miserable conditions by a late converted try to nil.

At the final whistle, the referee, England's Frank Potter-Irwin, experienced a fright as the crowd made a bee-line for him. This match was the first between the two nations since the notorious riot game of 1913 when the referee had been nearly lynched by the crowd. Consequently, the French press had issued an appeal to the spectators before the game, asking them to behave politely to the referee and France's Scottish guests.

For a moment, players and officials feared a repeat of the 1913 scenes as spectators closed on Mr Potter-Irwin. But to everyone's relief the enthusiasts' only purpose was to chair him from the ground in a show of sportsmanship that was greeted with applause.

FIRST FULL HOUSE

SWANSEA, JANUARY 1920

The first home international match after the first world war was staged at Swansea in January 1920, when Wales were hosts to England. It was the first meeting of the countries for six seasons, making it a very difficult match to call. Beforehand, predictions varied between a ten-point win and a ten-point defeat for the home side, but when the teams awoke on the morning of the match to a wet, windy day the pendulum swung firmly back in Wales's favour.

The prospects of playing the Welsh in difficult conditions clearly troubled the English selectors who, at the last moment, made a change to their original XV. Wilfrid Lowry, the Birkenhead Park wing, had actually appeared with the England XV for their customary team group photograph before it was decided that Harold Day of Leicester and the Army would be better suited to the conditions. Day played, scoring the try and kicking the conversion that made up England's five points.

Yet the man who grabbed the headlines on this occasion was a Welshman named Jerry Shea. A diminutive centre with a strong hand-off, Shea opened the scoring with a penalty goal into the wind and rain in the first half. Then came Day's efforts to send England into the interval nursing a slender two-point lead, 5–3.

Wales were back in front within five minutes of the restart, Shea dropping a goal. From this point the Welsh forwards took command and their backs, despite the treacherous state of the ground, began to revel. After 20 minutes, Shea exploited a chink in the English defence, broke through and, with a couple of swift changes of direction, ended up planting the ball behind the posts for a try that he easily converted.

At 12–5 all of Wales's points had been realised by Shea but the remarkable fact was that he had scored with every action: try, conversion, penalty and dropped goal. It was the first full house of scores achieved by a player in nearly fifty years of Test rugby. (Another thirty years would pass before Lewis Jones, playing for the Lions, would become the second player to perform one of the international game's rarest feats.)

Wick Powell scored a try for Wales before Shea brought the curtain down on his match-winning performance with a second dropped goal, to leave Wales comfortable winners by 19–5 over England.

The preoccupation with individual scoring records that is so commonplace nowadays was certainly less evident years ago. Jerry Shea's achievements that day, however, were given full coverage in the press. The *Sportsman* correctly concluded: 'The game will go down in Rugby history as [Shea's] match. Certainly he enjoyed a remarkable personal triumph [and] established a unique record.'

Others would not be so kind to the Newport man. He was severely criticised for his desire to achieve so much single-handed and, after a less convincing display against Scotland the next month, he was dropped. The methods of the brilliant individualist, it was felt, were incompatible with the Welsh style of back play 'in which self must practically disappear for the sake of combination'.

He played only once more for his country, in 1921 at Twickenham, before joining Wigan Rugby League club later the same year.

THE CROWD OVERSTEPS THE MARK

SWANSEA, FEBRUARY 1921

There have been international matches where the crowd rioted after the final whistle, occasions where the referee has had to shepherd crowds back from the touch-lines and there have even been Tests where captains have led their sides off the field temporarily in protest at refereeing decisions. But only once in a major international has the referee had to interrupt play to take the teams off the field because of the antics of spectators.

The occasion was the Wales-Scotland Five Nations match of 1921 played at St Helen's, Swansea. The match started promptly at 3.00 p.m. despite the problems caused by the record crowd, which resulted in spectators being allowed on to the grass in front of the terraces, bringing them fairly close to the touch-lines.

There was no sign of trouble until six minutes into the game when Wales were awarded a penalty. As Albert Jenkins prepared to take the kick, pandemonium broke out. A mass of spectators got to their feet and swarmed across the pitch, some 'committing disgraceful acts on the field of play'.

The police were unable to contain the crowd and the referee had no alternative but to halt the game. The players retreated to the pavilion for 15 minutes, during which time mounted police were called to clear the pitch. Wales appeared to be more discomfited by the disturbances than Scotland. When play resumed Jenkins missed his kick and the Scots, despite further stoppages for the referee and officials to persuade the encroaching crowds to retreat, coasted to an eleven-point lead before half-time.

Further crowd disturbances occurred during the interval and in the second half. For Wales, Jenkins landed two dropped goals and the Welsh backs engaged in an aerial bombardment of the Scottish goal, seeking a third which would have brought the home side the lead. (Such goals were valued at four points at this time.) But just as Wales appeared to be gaining the upper hand, the crowd again overstepped the lines and were lapping around the Scottish goal when the referee was again forced to stop play.

With patience the officials persuaded the crowd to settle, but when the game resumed it was Scotland who wrested the initiative from Wales and a late try sealed their first victory on Welsh soil for 29 years.

Never before, nor indeed since, have such disgraceful scenes been witnessed on an international ground.

TWO BLIND EYES

PARIS, JANUARY 1922

Rugby players were quick to join up to serve King and Country when, in August 1914, the war to end all wars began. Many clubs saw entire teams enlist and many were devastated by the effects of the war.

London Scottish was one of the clubs worst affected. On the last Saturday of the 1914 season the club fielded four senior XVs and all of those involved later joined the Exiles' regiment. Sadly only four returned in 1918 unaffected by their active service. All told, 69 of more than 200 of the club's playing members who served were killed in action. More than 50 were wounded and four were taken as prisoners of war, including Charles Usher who had played international rugby for Scotland in 1914.

Usher survived to lead his country after the war and took part in Scotland's first international of the 1920s, against France in Paris. Three players who appeared in that match had each lost an eye during the war: Scotland's prop, Jock Wemyss, and a couple of Frenchmen including Marcel Lubin-Lebrère who faced Wemyss in the scrums. At the after-match banquet the two struck up a great friendship which was to last for many years.

Arguably one of the most bizarre rugby matches occurred when these two men came up against each other again in the France-Scotland match two years later. Meeting before the match, the two old pals agreed to mark one another in the line-outs.

However, the two rugby Cyclopses had lost different eyes. As a result, in the line-outs along one touchline there was no problem as each was perfectly capable of keeping a beady eye on both the ball and one another. However, once play switched to the other touch-line, this was not the case and all hell broke loose as the old veterans barged, shoved and elbowed about, trying to feel their way through the line-outs.

Early in the game the referee's attention was drawn to the two men's blind-side antics. The official was a former England international, Dreadnought Harrison, who was a distinguished recent Services player. Charles Usher, who was now Scotland's captain, was another noted Services player and knew Harrison well.

'What's all this, Charles?' Harrison enquired after first observing Wemyss and Lubin-Lebrère conducting their own game within the game early in the first half. 'Just leave them,' Usher replied. 'It's a private arrangement; they're both half blind.'

Harrison got the message and left them to get on with it for the rest of the afternoon. The battle between the old soldiers was a microcosm of the match itself, the line-out count ending all square on a day when the sides drew 3-all.

TWO FREAK SCORES

TWICKENHAM, JANUARY 1923

Wales made their fifth visit to Twickenham in January 1923. And for the fifth time their journey was made in vain, England winning by a dropped goal and a try to a try: 7–3 under the scoring values then in vogue. This time, Wales could argue that they were particularly unlucky.

Never has a team achieved two such freak scores as England did on this occasion. The first came from the kick-off. A stiff breeze was blowing down the pitch when Wavell Wakefield kicked off into it for England. His kick went straight but, caught in the wind, the ball soared high before falling vertically into the path of Leo Price, the England flanker who was following up. Price ran on towards the Welsh 25 and, seeing his path blocked, took a drop at goal. Again the ball surged into the air, again it fell steeply from its highest point, and again Price was underneath it. This time he had only to canter half-a-dozen yards to touch down to the right of the posts.

England had scored a try ten seconds from the kick-off and before a Welshman had even touched the ball. 'Here was record breaking with a vengeance,' wrote Col Philip Trevor C.B.E. in the *Daily Telegraph*. 'It beat even the famous Adrian Stoop opening to the 1910 game. Much did the multitude indulge in anticipatory joy.'

But the thrill of the first minute did not last. The match settled into a dour struggle between two evenly-matched packs, though, when Wales scored a try six minutes later with the only constructive attacking movement of the match, at least it set up a tight and unpredictable battle. Wales then nearly went ahead when Joe Rees hit the upright with a drop shot, but England were happy to be level at half time.

The second fluke score, which brought the winning points, came five minutes from time after England, making better use of the wind than the Welsh, had been on the attack for most of the half.

Col Trevor again describes the action: '[Len] Corbett was standing a little in advance of the half-way line and about twenty yards from the touch-line when he got hold of the ball. One of the Welsh backs was practically on top of him at the time. He proceeded to do what a stodgy person will prefer to call the lucky, but which I shall take the liberty of calling the clever, thing. He passed the ball obliquely backwards through his legs to [Alastair] Smallwood [who] steadied himself for a fraction of a second and made the long [drop] shot. We seemed to wait an age for the result of the flight of that leisurely ball, but when it did come it was worth waiting for. It was the Tennysonian dénouement. It crossed the bar.'

HONEYMOON SWAN SONG

PARIS, APRIL 1923

Preparations for international matches were certainly different years ago as the following tale involving a former England Grand Slam captain illustrates.

W J A (he was always known as 'Dave') Davies was a Welsh-born outside half who played international rugby for England. His debut for England was in 1913 against the Second Springboks, when he made a favourable impression on the selectors in a 3–9 defeat. For the next ten years he was to remain the outstanding player in his position in England. In a career that brought him 22 caps, he was involved in four England Grand Slams and, after tasting defeat on that maiden appearance against South Africa, he never again featured on a losing England side.

His first season as captain was in 1921 when he steered England to a Grand Slam. The following year he was forced to stand down from the Wales match in Cardiff owing to injury. England lost 28–6 without him, but he returned to lead them unbeaten through the remaining three games of the campaign.

The 1923 season was to be his last before retirement from big time rugby. England duly proceeded to defeat Wales, Ireland and Scotland to claim the Triple Crown, leaving the game against France in Paris in April as the Grand Slam decider. Unfortunately, Davies, who was by then a Commander in the Navy, had arranged to marry his fiancée, Miss Peggy Waymouth of Southsea, shortly before this game.

He now had to make the decision as to whether he should

play in the match or depart on his honeymoon. Davies, however, had no intention of missing the important match and a solution was reached. The happy couple would take their honeymoon in Paris so that the groom could easily get to the Stade Colombes to lead his XV in their important match.

Mrs Davies wholeheartedly supported her husband. She enjoyed sport and was a keen tennis player herself and in later years, even after the death of her husband in 1967, was a knowledgeable rugby follower who regularly attended Twickenham internationals.

TRYING THE HIGH JUMP

TWICKENHAM, FEBRUARY 1924

Twickenham has enjoyed its fair share of famous tries: Prince Obolensky in 1936, Peter Jackson in 1958, Richard Sharp in 1963, and Andy Hancock in 1965, to mention four. But a couple of tries scored in the 1924 England-France match stand out as two of the more unusual witnessed at the ground.

England were playing a French XV that had been forced to make disruptive late changes when three of its leading players withdrew at the eleventh hour. The English side went ahead by 2–0, but there was a feeling among the crowd that their team was coasting. The match reports indicated a casualness in the home side's approach to the first half.

Then, just before the interval, came a blind-side England move that at last had the spectators on the edges of their seats. The half-backs, Arthur Young and Edward Myers, opened a gap to work Carston Catcheside clear on the right wing. Catcheside was not one of the fastest wings to play for England but when confronted by the French full-back, Laurent Pardo, a couple of yards from the goal line, he astounded everyone. Seeing his opponent stoop in preparation for a head-on tackle, Catcheside coolly high-jumped over Pardo and grounded the ball for a try as he landed.

At six-foot Pardo was one of the tallest full-backs in the Five Nations. Even the esteemed rugby correspondent of *The Times* was bemused. 'To jump over a big full-back's head – even though the latter be bending to make a low tackle – was an unexpected revelation,' he told his readers. Catcheside's move was catching. Towards the end of the match and with the score 19–4 in England's favour, the French right wing performed the same feat in the same corner of the ground. The second jump-try was scored by new cap Jacques Ballarin after he had cleared Bev Chantrill, the England full-back.

HM King George V was an interested spectator at the match and when introduced to Catcheside on a later Twickenham visit referred to the winger's flying try, adding a royal touch of disapproval at what he believed was a dangerous tactic.

Very dangerous, in fact. In 1899 a former New Zealand representative named Barney Armit had died performing the very same trick that Catcheside had perfected. Armit was playing for Otago against Taranaki when he was tipped over hurdling his opposite number. He landed heavily on the back of his head and broke his neck. Paralysed, he was taken to Dunedin hospital where he died from his injuries nearly 11 weeks later.

THREE PAIRS OF BROTHERS

CARDIFF, MARCH 1924

When Ireland beat Wales at Cardiff in March 1924 they created an unusual record by selecting three pairs of brothers in their XV. The Hewitts, Tom and Frank, were Belfast teenagers who masterminded the victory, each scoring a try. Then there were the Stephensons, George and Harry who were also from Belfast, playing in the threequarter line, and finally the Collopys, Dick and Billy from the Bective Rangers club in Dublin, who provided brute strength up front.

Frank Hewitt was only 17 and the youngest man to represent Ireland when he made his debut in this match. He sold two dummies on his way to scoring Ireland's third and decisive try in the second half. Earlier, his brother Tom had scored the first and the brothers Stephenson had combined to engineer the second of the scores.

But it was the younger Hewitt who captured the headlines for his performance in this match. 'Still a schoolboy, F S Hewitt will be able to look back upon his doings in this match with the utmost degree of personal satisfaction,' reported *Wisden's Rugby Football Almanack*.

BRONZE MEDAL . . .
JUST FOR TURNING UP

PARIS, MAY 1924

Rugby football was once an Olympic sport. In 1900, France, some six years before their first official cap international, beat Germany and Great Britain. The British team were selected mainly from Birmingham clubs and included only one capped player, a forward named Arthur Darby.

In 1908, Australia took the rugby Gold at the White City Olympics and in 1920, when the sport next featured at the Games, the United States beat France 8–0 in Antwerp. The Americans were bolstered by the presence of Morris Kirksey, one of their track stars who won Gold in the 4x100 metres relay as well as at rugby, making him one of the rare band who have collected winners' medals at two Olympic sports.

The reigning Olympic champions warmed up for the 1924 competition by playing matches in England where the accuracy and length of their American football-style throws at the line-out impressed opponents. Somewhat surprisingly, the players were not part of the official US Olympic party, but had to pay their own travel expenses and were even held up at Boulogne on the way to Paris by customs officials who queried the validity of their passports.

The Americans opened the defence of their Olympic title against Romania at Stade Colombes, where they experienced little difficulty in overcoming a side that had shipped more than 50 points against the French a week earlier. The American side adopted the New Zealand five-eight system behind the scrum, but packed down up front in the orthodox 3–2–3 system then familiar to British forwards. Their side was composed almost entirely of students from Stanford University in California and their superior speed and fitness were no match for the Romanians.

Only a tendency to over-elaborate in their handling prevented the Americans from running up more than a 37–0 victory. Frank Hyland in the centre and big Jack Patrick in the forwards were the outstanding players for the States, scoring seven tries between them. The referee was a Welshman named David Leyshon who had settled in France some years earlier.

The US then went on to beat France, who also beat the Romanians. But, despite these two defeats, the Romanians finished with the Bronze medal. Only three nations had entered the rugby tournament: Romania only had to turn up to ensure a medal – and it was the first Olympic honour Romania achieved in any sport.

Unsurprisingly, 1924 was the last year that rugby made an appearance as an official Olympic sport.

THE LAID BACK SAMOANS

APIA, AUGUST 1924

Rugby was brought to the Samoan islands by the Catholic Marist Brothers, but it was not until the arrival of New Zealanders in 1914 that the game was adopted as a national pastime. Until then, primitive matches had been played with empty coconut shells. The expatriates persuaded the New Zealand Rugby Union, whose support of Samoan rugby was a lifeline for more than two decades, to supply the islanders with proper leather balls and by 1924 Western Samoa was ready for its Test debut.

The laid back islanders entertained the touring Fijians in August at Apia. The legend has grown up that the game kicked off at 7.00 a.m. to enable the Samoans to get to work and that a large tree was situated on the half way line. The New Zealand rugby historian, Geoff Miller, who has researched the early days of Samoan Test rugby, confirms that the Samoans launched their international record with a 0–6 defeat by Fiji, but adds that the presence of a tree on the pitch was 'probably a myth'.

Even the reporting of early Test rugby on Western Samoa was pretty casual. Two years after their maiden Test they entertained the Tongans on Apia Park but, according to the *Samoa Times* of 6 August 1926, its rugby correspondent 'has failed us this week, and owing to a previous engagement at a hopscotch match near the Market Hall on the same afternoon we did not see the Rugby game'.

Nevertheless, despite the absence of a reporter, the newspaper announced that one of its own compositors had been present at the game and that he had reported that Tonga had won 14–5. Their man predicted, 'When Samoa goes down to Tonga next year the footballers of those flat islands will need the biggest tree in Nuku'alofa to hold the notches that will be needed to keep tally of Samoa's tries.' It all seems a long way from the electronic scoreboards of today's modern rugby stadia.

MOMENT THAT SILENCED TWICKENHAM

TWICKENHAM, JANUARY 1925

Like their predecessors of 1905, the All Blacks of 1924–5 arrived for their last international match of the British/Irish leg of their tour looking to preserve their unbeaten record. Between September and December 1924, a side led by Cliff Porter had won 27 matches before, in the New Year of 1925, they wound up their tour with a game against England at Twickenham. In 1905 it was Wales, as the holders of the Home Unions' Triple Crown, who lowered the All Blacks' flag. Twenty years on, it was England's turn as Triple Crown and Grand Slam holders, to offer the last resistance to the tourists.

Until the 1930s, the All Blacks packed down in a diamond formation at the scrums. There were two hookers up front who swung their outside feet inwards to kick rather than heel the put-in back through a scrum that was backed by three second-row men and locked by two men in the back-row. Because the ball whizzed back through the scrum under this arrangement, a scrum-half to put the ball in as well as an eighth man or rover who used to crouch behind the forwards awaiting the heel, were deployed on the fringes.

In Britain the norm was to pack down with three men in the front row: two props supporting a hooker in the middle. Reg Edwards, the Newport prop and captain, had disrupted the All Blacks in their match at Rodney Parade earlier in the tour by taking his front row one step aside as the packs were engaging for scrums, thereby giving his team not one but two loose heads. The New Zealanders, who were going to have none of this, had to take matters into their own hands in order to scrape home against the Welshmen by 13–10.

Edwards was also a seasoned England international (Newport being affiliated to both the English and Welsh Unions) and was chosen for their showdown with the visitors. A record Twickenham attendance of 60,000 packed its stands and terraces on an overcast day. The match, played on a heavy ground, started ferociously with Mr Freethy, the Welsh referee who had also controlled the tour match at Newport, having to sternly lecture both packs for their over-vigorous play. Edwards was again causing the New Zealand front row some problems in the set-scrums and his scrum-capped bald pate was clearly seen at the centre of several exchanges between the packs.

Mr Freethy spoke to the forwards three times in the opening six minutes and warned them that the next transgressor he saw would be dismissed. After ten minutes a line-out degenerated into another fracas and there was a shrill blast of the Welshman's whistle whereupon Cyril Brownlie, one of the New Zealand forwards, was sent off. The crowd fell stunned. Reports say that you could have heard a pin drop as the incredulous crowd watched the crestfallen Brownlie trudge off the field. Embarrassed players – there but for the grace of God went they – fiddled with their kit uneasily as they absorbed the enormity of the occasion. Never before had a player been given his marching orders in an international. And to think it had happened at Twickenham. The Prince of Wales, the future Edward VIII, was a spectator at the match and pleaded in vain at half-time for the New Zealander to be allowed back.

Brownlie's second-row colleagues that afternoon were his brother Maurice and big Read Masters, who later published his diary of the tour. His first-hand description of the event is worth re-telling: 'Through the over-keenness of one of England's forwards – who had also adopted illegal tactics in a previous game – heated play was in evidence in the first and many subsequent scrums,' he wrote. 'Thrice the referee issued a general warning to both packs and appealed for calmer play.

Then came the climax. After some loose play following a line-out, the whistle sounded, followed by the remark, "You go off."

'Our horror can be imagined when we realised that the remark was directed at Cyril Brownlie,' Masters continued. 'Cyril, without a word, left the field [but] never in my life have I experienced anything like the weird silence that fell over Twickenham as he walked away.'

The teams settled down to play a classic match thereafter. A man short, New Zealand rose to the occasion bravely, their forwards playing like men possessed. Maurice Brownlie, in particular, was a tower of strength in the midst of the depleted All Blacks' pack. With a clear point to make, he scored one of the four tries that helped the New Zealanders build an impressive 17–3 lead. England staged a worthy recovery in the last 20 minutes of the match when the visitors, no doubt exhausted at playing for so long with only 14 men, relaxed. At the end, though, New Zealand emerged with their invincible record intact: England 11, New Zealand 17.

BACK TO SQUARE ONE

TWICKENHAM, JANUARY 1927

Media coverage of international rugby took a giant leap forward in January 1927 when Captain Teddy Wakelam, a former Harlequins player, provided the first live radio commentary of any British sporting event.

The BBC was planning to broaden its scope and keen to adopt the American custom of relaying outside broadcasts of major sporting occasions. Out of the blue, Wakelam was telephoned and asked if he would undergo a microphone test. The former player jumped at the opportunity and within a couple of weeks was perched in a precarious position in the south-west corner of Twickenham, providing commentary on the England-Wales international. The only advice given to him was 'Don't swear.'

A day or two before making his maiden broadcast he had visited the ground with a BBC production team to carry out a reconnaissance, and it was during the discussions that the idea of using a plan of the field divided into eight equal squares was formed. These squares were numbered and as the commentator described the play, his assistant would announce in the background: 'Square three, square two . . . and back to square one.' The *Radio Times* and Saturday newspapers used to carry the plan of the ground showing the squares, so that those listening at home could follow the game while the commentator was free to concentrate on the names of players and the passages of play.

The experiment was generally well received and the BBC

decided to retain Wakelam for the remainder of that season and for many more after it. Rugby was thus brought immediately into the households of those who were unable to attend matches and followers of the game no longer had to rely on newspaper accounts to discover what had happened.

Bernard Darwin, a columnist for *The Times*, reviewed the original broadcast favourably, adding with insight: 'In the course of time all sports and leading outdoor events will be so reported.'

AN ELIGIBILITY ROW

MASTERTON, JULY 1927

The Ranfurly Shield was for many years the only tangible prize for which New Zealand's provincial sides regularly did battle. The Shield, known affectionately as the Log o' Wood and given by the Governor of New Zealand in 1902, is held on a challenge basis with the provinces taking turns to beat the holders. Matches always take place on the holders' ground.

Hawke's Bay were the undisputed champion side of New Zealand in the 1920s. After taking the Shield off Wellington in August 1922, they established a record by beating off the challenges of 24 provinces over a five-year period before finally succumbing in June 1927 to Wairarapa.

A month later, the Bay were challenging to regain their title. The match in Masterton was memorable for events off the field as well as on it. More than 10,000 were present on the Solway Showgrounds to see a titanic struggle between two sides packed with All Black representatives. The battle for vantage points among the spectators was pretty fierce and a number who clambered on to a groundsman's shed for a clear view of the match were injured when it collapsed under their weight.

The battle on the field was even fiercer, with referee Bert McKenzie having to rule the match with a rod of iron. The Bay's captain Maurice Brownlie and Wairarapa's Quintin Donald, both distinguished All Black forwards, were sent off during a game that Hawke's Bay won 21–10, thereby regaining the Shield. Or so they thought.

Wairarapa, however, had other ideas and contested the

result. Before the match the Hawke's Bay selectors had scoured their region for players. The result of their combing was that Wattie Barclay, who had led the Maoris on a tour of Britain and France six months earlier, was called up to play in the Bay's threequarter line. Indeed, after Brownlie's dismissal he took over as captain of the side.

Although a former Hawke's Bay representative, Barclay had played a couple of games for Auckland earlier in the season, a fact that did not escape the Wairarapa committee. Consequently, they made an appeal to the New Zealand Rugby Football Union for the province to retain the Shield on the grounds that the opposition had fielded an ineligible player. The qualification period for provincial players was three weeks' domicile, so they argued that Barclay, having only recently returned to the Hawke's Bay area, was not a *bona fide* resident. The NZRFU agreed with this argument and the Shield was duly restored to Wairarapa.

THE FOREGONE CONCLUSION

CARTERTON, AUGUST 1929

Wairarapa began a long series of Ranfurly Shield victories with an 8–7 victory over Canterbury in July 1928. They then successfully defended the Shield through eight challenges before facing Southland at the Carterton Showgrounds on 31 August, 1929. The match was the hundredth of the Shield series, and the holders were so confident of another victory that they didn't even bother to arrange for the Log o' Wood to be brought the 20 or so miles from Masterton, where it was on display in the shop window of Bert Cooke's mercery business. Cooke, the outstanding New Zealand centre of the 1920s and the holders' captain, was one of eleven All Blacks in the side.

By contrast, Southland had only four New Zealand representatives. Moreover, three of their best players failed to arrive in time for the kick-off. But the strong favourites received a jolt in the first 20 minutes as Gil Porter kicked a goal from a mark, a penalty and dropped a goal to put the visitors 10–0 ahead. Wairarapa were stale: they had become a side whose over-confidence was to prove its undoing. Southland led 13–6 at the pause and finished 19–16 – winners with Porter kicking 13 of their points.

It then dawned on the officials that there was no trophy to present. A Wairarapa official was hastily despatched to retrieve the Shield from Bert Cooke's shop so that it could be presented to the new champions.

The whole province of Wairarapa went into mourning and its MP, George Sykes, received a telegram in the New Zealand

Parliament which read, 'Deepest sympathies in your sad bereavement.'

After the disappointment of their foregone conclusion, Wairarapa had to wait more than 20 years before briefly holding the Shield again.

LAST-MINUTE TEAM CHANGE

CARDIFF, JANUARY 1930

Sam Tucker of Bristol was the outstanding hooker of the 1920s. He was one of the first Englishmen to specialise in the position, it being common up to the Great War for forwards to pack down in scrum formation simply in the order that they arrived: the so-called First Up, First Down arrangement.

Tucker had already won 22 caps and had helped England to a Grand Slam when, at the start of the 1930 Five Nations Championship, he was dropped from the England side to meet Wales in Cardiff. The England selectors were looking for a fast, fit eight to take on the Welsh and named an experimental pack in which five players were new caps.

On the eve of the match, prop Henry Rew stubbed his toe in training at Penarth. On the morning of the game it transpired that his injury was worse than originally diagnosed and he had to withdraw from the side. Faced with several options, the Rugby Football Union's secretary, Sydney Cooper, telephoned Sam Tucker's Bristol office at 12.25 p.m. and, finding the former hooker at his desk, demanded that Tucker get himself to Cardiff pretty damned quick.

Tucker managed to arrange a flight from nearby Filton Aerodrome and, after picking up his kit, took a taxi and boarded a two-seater bi-plane at 1.50. In his own words, Tucker 'was in an open cockpit with what looked to me like a bit of fuselage and a few pieces of wire between me and eternity'. Ten minutes into his maiden flight he was over Cardiff and, after circling around, the pilot landed in a field on the outskirts of the city. Tucker hitched a lift in a coal lorry to the city centre where his next problem was to gain entry to the ground.

A huge crowd had turned up at the gates to see the match. In those days internationals at Cardiff were not all-ticket affairs and it was a matter of first come, first served, as far as admittance to the ground was concerned. Eventually, Tucker managed to talk his way in and arrived in the changing room at 2.40, five minutes before kick-off time. He played hooker with Dave Kendrew, the originally selected hooker, moving to prop. Tucker had a blinder and kept his place in the side for the rest of a season in which England carried off the Five Nations title.

For last-minute call-ups Sam Tucker's adventure was unique. But spare a thought for poor Norman Matthews, the Bath and Bridgwater prop who was an England travelling reserve for that Cardiff game. The England selectors, thinking that Tucker had failed to arrange transport, had decided that Matthews would take Henry Rew's place in the front-row. Matthews was actually ready changed into an England jersey when Tucker turned up breathless at the dressing room door. Matthews never got to wear an England jersey again: a case of so near, so close and so unlucky.

SCORES BEFORE AND AFTER TIME

CARDIFF, FEBRUARY 1931

Many international matches have gone to the wire with the deciding score coming in injury time at the end of a see-saw match. But, when Wales and Scotland met at Cardiff in 1931, there were scores before the published kick-off time as well as in stoppage time at the end of the match.

The match programme and tickets printed for the game showed that the kick-off was scheduled for 3.00 p.m. But the early arrival of a capacity crowd on a warm spring-like afternoon prompted the authorities to bring forward the start time by five minutes.

Wales, making first use of a stiff breeze, took the lead after a clever reverse pass by their scrum-half, Wick Powell, sent Harry Bowcott on a run at the Scottish backs. Tommy Jones-Davies, his centre, made a classic cut-through and drew the Scottish defence before feeding on to Claud Davey, who exploited the overlap to send Jack Morley haring over in the right corner. Wales were thus three points up in as many minutes, the clock showing 2.58 . . . two minutes before the official start time.

The match developed into the best game of the season's Five Nations Championship. Despite the early setback, Scotland's forwards forced the pace and laid the foundations for the visitors to get back into the game. A kick ahead by Max Simmers caught the Welsh defence at sixes and sevens and new cap Donald Crichton-Miller, following up at speed, dribbled the ball over the Welsh line for an equalising score.

Early in the second half, Crichton-Miller who, like a good flanker was here, there and everwhere throughout the match, was up in support when a jinking run by Phil MacPherson seemed to founder on the rock-like defence of the Welsh full-back and captain, Jack Bassett. Bassett's tackle, though, was not effective enough to prevent MacPherson from slipping the ball to his flanker and the try, converted by Jock Allan, put Scotland 8–3 ahead.

There was nothing to suggest on the evidence of the first hour's play that Wales would overcome this deficit. The handling of their backs had been weak and Bowcott had been swapped with Jones-Davies in an attempt to bring a sharper attacking edge to the Welsh backs. At length their forwards rallied and accurate Welsh back play at last succeeded in opening up the Scottish defence. Wales decamped to the Scottish 25 and, after stretching the Scottish backs from right to left and back again, Wales finally scored when Watcyn Thomas, despite carrying a fractured collar-bone from an earlier tackle, forced his way over for a try at the posts. Jack Bassett converted and the crowd steeled itself for a tense finish.

Play now fluctuated in a simple harmonic motion between the goal-lines. Scotland's backs still seemed the more confident handling the ball, but it was Wales's pack who were providing the gilt-edged possession. As the clock advanced to show that more than 40 minutes of play had passed in the second half, the crowd became resigned to accepting that the match would end as an eight-all draw.

Then, in the second minute of time added on for stoppages, there was a fluke score. A Welsh attack foundered when a pass to Bowcott struck his chest, rebounded to a Scotsman and in turn cannoned off sideways. Ronnie Boon, ever an opportunist, came in smartly off the left wing and hacked the loose ball towards the Scottish line. His quick thinking caught the Scots unaware and Boon's pace enabled him to win the race for the touchdown and an extra time winning score.

Wales went on to win the Championship title although

many agreed that a draw would have been a fair result. In the context of Wales-Scotland matches it would also have been a unique result: in more than one hundred years of competition Wales and Scotland have never shared a draw on Welsh soil.

FRENCH OUTCASTS

PARIS, APRIL 1931

For a number of years during the 1920s there had been growing unease in the four Home Unions about the conduct of the game in France. There were suggestions that the intense rivalry of their well organised championship had led to a state whereby several French clubs were being subsidised and controlled in an irregular manner. A number of French clubs were at odds with their own Union and often refused to release players to the national side when big club championship matches were looming.

Matters were brought to a head in early 1931 when a dozen French clubs broke away from their federation to form their own alliance. Such recalcitrance was unacceptable to the Home Unions who, at their meeting of 13 February on the eve of the England-Ireland match at Twickenham, passed a resolution that stated that matches would not be resumed with the French until 'the control and conduct of the game [in France] has been placed on a satisfactory basis'. No slur was meant on the French Federation who, indeed, did all in its power in the months that followed to put the game in France in order. The British felt that there were elements to the split that were reminiscent of the break with England's northern clubs some forty years earlier, which had led to the formation of the professional Northern Union which later became the Rugby League.

But the timing of the announcement was crass, for the French were thus given notice of their ejection from the Five Nations championship before they had finished playing all their games in the current tournament. It is hard to imagine the feelings among the two fifteens of France and England, let alone the respective committees of the two countries' Rugby Unions, as they convened for the game in Paris on Easter Monday and attended the after-match function.

In its preview of the game *The Times*, understanding the climate in which the match would take place, declared: 'It would be a pity if ill-considered criticisms of British motives incited a holiday crowd to make a demonstration and so upset both teams, who can be relied upon to do their best to improve instead of embitter a rather awkward situation.'

The hopes were largely upheld and in the end rugby football triumphed over politics as the two sides engaged in an exciting match. True, there was a roar of derision when England emerged from their dressing room and the crowd booed them for most of the match. Three times England held the lead before France, through an unexpected drop at goal by Georges Gérald which just scraped over the crossbar, snatched a 14–13 victory. France rejoiced so much at their victory that dark thoughts over being cast out of the Five Nations were temporarily cast aside.

At the after-match function the England captain, Carl (later Sir Carl) Aarvold thanked the French players for a sporting match, revealed that he had always enjoyed playing against them and expressed a wish soon to be doing so again. He was given a standing ovation by his hosts.

The truth was, though, that France had played their last international fixture against a British or Irish XV for nine long years.

A PAIR OF FIVES

TWICKENHAM, JANUARY 1932 AND PARIS, OCTOBER 1999

When Jannie de Beer dropped five goals for South Africa against England in the Stade de France, Paris, in the 1999 Rugby World Cup quarter-finals everyone marvelled at the feat. No-one could even remember a player taking five such kicks at goal before, let alone finding the target on every occasion.

De Beer had only been drafted into the Springboks' squad relatively late that season, having thought that his international career was done and dusted. But his kicks, in the third, fifth, 13th, 31st and 34th minutes of the second half of the match, effectively provided the difference between two teams who were hell-bent on winning and reaching the semi-finals of the World Cup. The score had been only 16–15 to South Africa early in the second half when de Beer's aerial bombardment started. Realising that the drop was the only scoring method that England could not defend against, de Beer ruthlessly exploited one of the game's oldest arts. By the time he had finished drop-kicking to his heart's content the score was 31–21 and the Springboks were home and dry.

Now, tucked away in the files of past England-South Africa contests is the account of the 1932 match at Twickenham. South Africa won that game 7–0 in the days when scoring was less prolific. But the press reports of that match show that de Beer was by no means the first player to attempt five dropped goals in a match.

The South African captain of 1932 was Bennie Osler, a deadly kicker whether punting tactically for touch, placing goals or drop-kicking. But at Twickenham his mastery of the drop temporarily escaped him.

South Africa won a wealth of possession from the set scrums and line-outs, but Osler's dour tactics meant that rarely were his threequarters brought into the game. 'No fly-half can ever have had the ball so regularly in an international match and done so little with it,' reported Howard Marshall. Osler's safety first methods reduced the game to little more than a kicking spectacle for the big crowd and the only try of the game came in the first half when, after 15 minutes, Ferdie Bergh followed up a speculative kick ahead from a line-out and dived on the ball to score.

It was in the second half – like de Beer 67 years later – that Osler took his pots at goal. Also like de Beer, the South African captain had decided that the only scoring action England could not defend against was the one that placed the ball over their heads. Five times he dropped for goal, but unlike de Beer five times he missed.

Ironically the final scoring action was a dropped goal. But not one kicked by Osler. His full-back was another prodigious kicker named Gerry Brand. Two minutes from time, Brand caught the ball near touch on half-way and, into the wind, sent the ball sailing high over the bar with the longest dropped goal ever recorded in an international match.

THE OVER-INFLATED BALL

CARDIFF, MARCH 1932

Many players have been caught out by the perverse bounce of the oval rugby ball. Over-inflate it and the ball will play all manner of tricks, particularly on a firm ground, as both Ireland and Wales (to their cost) found in a Championship decider played on a sunny, early-spring afternoon in Cardiff in March 1932.

Wales had beaten England and Scotland and retained an unchanged fifteen for their Triple Crown clash against an Irish side that had secured a decisive win over Scotland but lost narrowly by 11–8 at home to England. There was little to choose between the sides on paper and, as it turned out, there was little to choose between them on the field of play.

From an early stage of the match it was apparent that the ball was over-inflated but the referee made no attempt to have it changed. Shaun Waide kicked ahead but was robbed of a try in the follow-up when the ball bounced eccentrically into touch. Ireland eventually opened the scoring with a try after ten minutes, but Wales equalised when Claud Davey went over and it was 3–3 at the interval.

Ireland's second try put them 6–3 ahead before Dickie Ralph dropped a goal on the hour to put Wales in front for the first time in the match. The ball's perversity led to Ireland's next score. Eugene Davy attempted to drop a goal for Ireland but sent the ball wide. The experienced Welsh full-back and captain, Jack Bassett, ordered his colleague, Ronnie Boon, to stand aside and leave the ball for his attention. But the full-back completely misjudged its flight, the ball hit his arm and ballooned to Ned Lightfoot on Ireland's right wing who gratefully accepted his gift and scored.

Moments later Wales were presented with the chance to regain the lead when, under pressure, Ernie Ridgeway, Ireland's full-back, failed to find touch from his own goal line. It was ten to one on that Jack Morley would gather it on the Welsh right and dot the ball down in the corner. But once more the ball bobbed like a cork on troubled waters to play tricks on Wales. Instead of gathering it, Morley saw Shaun Waide snaffle it up and set off on an eighty yards run past Jack Bassett for a try that put his side 12–7 ahead. For the fourth time in four attempts, Ireland's place-kicking with the lively ball let them down as the conversion went wide.

Wales rallied and Dickie Ralph threaded his way through a forest of defenders for the best solo try of the match. Bassett's conversion with the final kick of the afternoon could still have saved the game for Wales and won them the International Championship title. But the over-blown leather again confounded the Welsh. The captain's kick veered away from the posts at the last minute, Wales were left to share the title with Ireland, and poor old Jack Bassett, one of Wales's finest full-backs of all time, was dropped and never forgiven for a match in which, all along, the ball had been at fault, playing its tricks on one and all.

THE WRONG SCORE

TWICKENHAM, JANUARY 1933

Wales had already made nine fruitless journeys to the Rugby Football Union's Twickenham headquarters when an experimental side that was a mix of experienced forwards and youthful backs travelled from the Principality to London for the opening match of the 1933 International Championship. Many of Wales's defeats at the ground had been near things and over the years a myth had developed in South Wales that Twickenham was their bogey ground.

High hopes were pinned on a 19-year-old leggy centre from North Wales named Wilf Wooller who was among the seven Welsh newcomers. The teenager enjoyed a successful debut. He was given few opportunities to show his strides in attack but his magnificent side-on tackling, especially in the second half, had the required effect of reducing the danger posed by England's centres.

Even so, England opened the scoring when Don Burland broke through in the first half to send Walter Elliot in for a try. Soon after the interval, however, Wales took the lead when wing threequarter Ronnie Boon dropped a goal from a loose maul 20 yards from the English posts. That put Wales 4–3 ahead with all to play for. The Welsh pack began to exercise a hold on their opponents, though only Wooller's tackle at the corner flag prevented Elliot from restoring England's lead after a 30-yard chase.

Then Ronnie Boon put Wales further ahead with a try that was followed by a most unusual incident. Welsh centre Claude

Davey drew the English full-back perfectly to release Boon on a run that took the wing arcing outside the defence for a try near the posts. Viv Jenkins, making his Welsh debut despite nursing a high fever, lined up the simple kick and sent the ball, so the Welsh supporters and Welsh touch judge thought, straight between the posts. Even the scoreboard operator believed that the kick was good, for he marked up a Welsh lead of 9–3 with time running out. Converted tries were worth only five points at this time, so most of the crowd and probably the players, too, felt that Wales were virtually safe with England having to score twice to win.

That, however, was not so. Only at the end of the match was it made clear by the Irish referee, Tom Bell, that Jenkins's conversion kick from close range had failed. It was true that Mr Llewellyn, the Welsh touch judge, had signalled a goal. He was from Bridgend, Jenkins's home club, and presumably could not believe that the young place kicker would miss a kick from such a good position.

The score had come ten minutes from no-side and the misunderstanding could have had a profound influence on the outcome of the match. The fact was that England only needed another breakaway try and conversion to win the match. Whether or not the English players were aware of the position is not recorded, though it was reported that the Welsh forwards so dominated the closing stages of the match that it was as much as England could do to prevent Wales from increasing their lead.

A similar incident in the Paris international between France and Scotland in 1951 might have had more serious consequences. A French conversion attempt on the stroke of half-time was touched in flight by a Scotsman and therefore disallowed by the referee. But the Stade Colombes scoreboard operator, Jacques Robin, credited his side with the two points after an announcer had given the score as 8–6 to France instead of 6–6.

The second half was a see-saw affair and with five minutes remaining Scotland actually led 12–11 while the scoreboard showed France ahead 13–12. The referee was the well-known English official Tom Pearce, who had earlier communicated the correct score to the marker in the score box. The 30-year-old Monsieur Robin, however, deliberately ignored requests to change the scores, despite pleas from the French officials as well as from the referee.

'I was afraid of trouble from the crowd if I corrected the scoreboard,' he told reporters later. 'I was waiting for the loudspeaker to announce the correction, but it remained silent,' he added.

Fortunately a major incident was avoided when Jean Prat landed what turned out to be France's winning points from a penalty goal only three minutes from time. British journalists attending the match were unanimous in siding with the score-marker's view, noting that the French crowd was the most partisan seen since the war.

THE VERY INEXPERIENCED TEAM

CARDIFF, JANUARY 1934

Ask the average follower to nominate international rugby's most fickle selection panel and to a man they would answer, France. In the 1960s and 1970s the French selectors were notorious for their chopping and changing, even of successful teams. When they won their first Grand Slam in 1968, for example, they called on no fewer than 27 players. Moreover, after winning their first two matches of that campaign they made nine changes for their home game with England. It prompted some amusing ironic headlines in later years. 'France make only eight changes,' announced one newspaper a year later when the guillotine fell on the XV that lost against England at Twickenham.

Yet the most fickle international selection of all time was not the result of Gallic shrugs nor even of cool Anglo-Saxon logic at a time when English teams were regularly put through the mill in the early 1970s. Instead, the credit for chopping up an entire fifteen goes to the Welsh Big Five who, in January 1934, for the game against England at Cardiff, fielded a side that showed fifteen changes from the fifteen who had finished the previous season in Belfast.

Welsh rugby had started 1933 with seven new caps and a first ever win at Twickenham. There were high hopes in the Principality that at last a fifteen was coming together that would put Welsh rugby back on top of the Championship table with a first Triple Crown success since 1911. Alas, defeat at home to Scotland was followed by a 10–5 loss in Ireland. There

114

had, however, been high jinx on the boat across to Belfast for that match. Several Welsh players hit the booze hard during the voyage, and one had to empty a couple of bottles of beer down the sink of his cabin when a member of the Welsh committee paid him an unexpected visit. Subsequently, Watcyn Thomas, the Welsh captain whose strong leadership had played such an important part in the Twickenham win, was relieved of the captaincy at the end of the season and never again appeared in a Welsh fifteen despite impressing the 1935 All Blacks as the best all-round forward they met.

But even so, nobody would have predicted that the selectors would start with an absolutely clean sheet when they sat down to choose the team to open the 1934 season against England. In those days the Welsh staged three official trials before naming their first international side of the season. The first took place at Llanelli where, no doubt to the selectors' satisfaction, their Probables defeated the Possibles by the convincing margin of 29–16. Even so, the writing was already on the wall: only Viv Jenkins (full-back) and Maurice Turnbull (scrum-half) from the side that played in Belfast, played for the Probables in the trial.

Turnbull was then dropped for the second trial, at Newport, and after the final trial at Cardiff the selectors named a dozen new caps for the England match. The side was described as 'more of an Anglo-Welsh side than any which ever before has represented Wales'. All told, there were nine University students, Service men or exiles in the team that was originally selected. When Jenkins withdrew with a pulled leg muscle, the selectors brought in a thirteenth new cap in Bryn Howells of Llanelli, leaving Claud Davey (centre) and Dai Thomas (lock) as the only previously capped players in the side. In addition, no two of its pack had ever played alongside each other before.

Not surprisingly, Wales lost 9–0 and the selectors were castigated. Their experiments were seen as no more than pure folly.

THE FULL-BACK WHO FLOUTED CONVENTION

SWANSEA, MARCH 1934

The introduction in 1968–9 of the so-called Australian dispensation law which restricted direct kicking into touch to within the defending side's 25 had far-reaching effects. International matches were opened up and the role of the full-back, formerly the last line of defence, radically changed. Full-backs became attacking weapons and tries scored by number 15s increased like the proverbial mustard seed in the following years.

But for the first half of the twentieth century, the job description of the full-back was to tackle, catch safely and kick to touch. Then, in 1934, one player showed the way ahead by flouting convention to become the first from his position to score a try in the International Championship.

His name was Vivian Jenkins of Bridgend. He had learned the game at Llandovery College before going up to Oxford University, where he won three Blues as a strong attacking centre between 1930 and 1932. He had been expected to enter the Welsh side of 1933 in his Varsity position but had converted to full-back at the behest of the Welsh selectors for the final trial that season. He was to become the outstanding player in Britain in his position during the 1930s.

The match with Ireland at Swansea in 1934 had been running for more than hour before Jenkins's moment of history arrived. The Irish, who had had the better of the match, twice came within an ace of scoring in the first half but, as the game entered its final ten minutes, the teams remained deadlocked.

116

An Irish kick deep into Welsh territory was fielded on his own 25 by Jenkins, who initiated an attack. Showing the skills that made him such an effective centre at Oxford he gained 30 yards before passing to Idwal Rees the Welsh right centre. Rees took play into the Irish 25 where, faced by the defending full-back, he passed out to Arthur Bassett, his wing. The cover managed to race across, but as Bassett was smothered into touch he released the ball in-field where Jenkins, who had followed up instinctively behind his threequarters, was at hand to pick up and calmly cross for a try which he converted from a wide angle. Wales scored twice more in the next five minutes to finish winners by the rather flattering margin of 13–0.

The Welsh full-back's action caused an outcry among some sections of the rugby fraternity. The purists argued that it was not the done thing for a full-back to score a try, especially in an international. Instead, they claimed, Jenkins should have followed the coaching manual and booted the ball into touch when he first received it. Suffice it to say that no full-back scored a try in the Championship again until 1962.

ALL BLACKS BEATEN BY SCHOOLBOYS

SWANSEA, SEPTEMBER 1935

Official New Zealand teams had played 67 matches on European soil and lost just once (to Wales by a try to nil in 1905) when the Third All Blacks of 1935 arrived at Swansea to play the All Whites in the fifth match of their tour.

The day was one that west Wales folk are familiar with, a persistent drizzle coming in off the sea from mid-afternoon until dusk. These were conditions which Old Stager, Welsh rugby's leading critic of the day, had referred to whilst staring into his crystal ball when preparing his morning of the match preview: 'With heavy going and a greasy ball the tourists may be less convincing. Our visitors may meet with an unpleasant surprise if they run against one of the best Welsh sides [Swansea] in foul weather.'

But the weather wasn't the only factor that would surprise the All Blacks. Swansea's half-backs were Willie Davies and Haydn Tanner, Gowerton cousins who had been the pivotal point of a successful All Whites' XV since the previous September. These two were in the best Welsh half-back traditions: quick-witted, sure of foot and brilliant individualists who could also function intelligently as part of the team. Neither had yet played for Wales, but within the space of six months both would win their caps.

The cousins revealed sound tactical judgement from early on in the match, playing with sureness and at the same time weighing up their famous opponents. Their constant probing

118

runs worried the All Blacks and gave confidence to a Swansea pack that soon began to hold its own up front.

It was from a forward drive that Swansea opened the scoring. The New Zealanders were forced to concede a line-out and from the throw-in Dennis Hunt scrambled over. Thereafter the match was always thrilling and contained many movements which, in the words of another Welsh correspondent, 'permitted real rugby lovers to drink deeply of the champagne of the game'. The first glass of bubbly was a Swansea vintage. Willie Davies, who was varying his game cleverly, completely tricked the visitors' defence with a jinking run and opened a huge gap for Claud Davey to stride 30 yards unchallenged for a try that Wilf Harris converted.

New Zealand pulled back three points with a Nelson Ball try, but before half-time the Swansea halves had engineered another score. Davies again sent the New Zealand defence the wrong way and once again Davey was the beneficiary, bringing the score to 11–3 at the interval.

It was then that the weather set in and, during a second half that produced no further scoring, the Swansea forwards, matching the bigger New Zealanders in the heavy conditions, made victory possible. But it was the halves who had made it certain, as the tourists' captain, Jack Manchester, acknowledged at the after-match reception.

'Haydn Tanner and Willie Davies gave a wonderful performance,' he said, 'but please don't tell them back home in New Zealand that we were beaten by a pair of schoolboys.'

Indeed, Tanner and Davies were schoolboys, both being in their last term at Gowerton County School at the time of this first ever defeat of New Zealand by a British club side.

FIRE BRIGADE HOSES CROWD

CARDIFF, MARCH 1936

The 1936 Wales-Ireland match was quite simply the game everyone wanted to see. Unbeaten Ireland were seeking their first Triple Crown since 1899, while Wales, who had earlier in the season beaten the All Blacks by a point, could win the International Championship by beating the Irish.

The whole of Wales and most of Ireland descended on Cardiff on Saturday 14 March to witness the match of the season. Internationals were not all-ticket affairs in those days and the crowds admitted to many rugby grounds for championship deciders or tour matches would make modern day officials with responsibility for crowd safety wince in disbelief. At many matches spectators were put under severe stress by the crushes created from overcrowding on the terraces. However, never before (nor indeed since) did the authorities take matters into their hands to the same degree as the Cardiff Fire Brigade did on this early spring day in 1936.

Long before the 3.30 kick-off the ground was full. Queues had formed in Westgate Street at breakfast time even though the gates did not open until 11.30 a.m. By 1.00 p.m., two and a half hours before the kick-off, the gates were closed. Some of the huge crowds locked out, however, burst through a police cordon at one of the ground's main entrances and thousands poured on to the terraces.

Later, a further and potentially more dangerous influx of people onto the terraces was prevented by the actions of the Cardiff Fire Brigade. A boat train of Irish supporters had arrived from Fishguard after the Westgate Street entrance had been shut and, on finding they were not going to be allowed into the ground, the angry late arrivals began scaling the gates to get in. It was then that the Cardiff Fire Brigade sprang into action, turning their hoses on the miscreants to deter them. The measure was successful and the invaders withdrew, their spirits suitably dampened, and a major disaster was probably averted.

Even so, when the match began, more than 70,000 were estimated to be present. The crush was so intense that a 60-year-old man from Trealaw near Pontypridd collapsed and died in the ground, a Newport man was detained in hospital suffering from concussion, 18 received minor injuries and the St John's Ambulancemen were kept busy during the match as more than 200 walking wounded sought attention.

Under these conditions, the patience of the players and of the referee, Mr Cyril Gadney of England, were severely tested before the match could be completed. Sensing the danger to lives from the huge crushes on the terraces, policemen helped those who were pinned to the enclosure fencing onto the field. The move prompted a surge of other spectators to jump over and crowd the touch lines and goal lines. As a result, when play settled at the west end of the ground, those packed behind the east goal trespassed infield, and vice versa.

On several occasions the match had to be interrupted for spectators to be cleared from the field of play. Photographs of the match show the Welsh touch-judge, Lot Thorn of Penarth, having to patrol his line from inside the field of play as spectators more than a dozen deep lapped over from the old north enclosure. Players throwing in to lineouts were handed the ball by supporters standing literally at their elbows. It was a tribute to the teams and Mr Gadney that the game was completed.

The match itself was an exciting one in which no quarter was asked and none given. The Welsh forwards played above themselves, surprising the visiting Irish pack who were expected to carry all before them. The conditions were ideal for running rugby, but the tension of the occasion dictated that tactics should be kept tight and the only score of the match was a penalty goal kicked by Viv Jenkins for Wales in the twentieth minute of the first half.

WARTIME CAPS IN PARIS

PARIS, FEBRUARY 1940

The 1939–40 rugby season promised to be the most significant one of the decade. A full-scale tour of Britain by the Wallabies was scheduled to start in September and, with playing relations renewed with France, a full Five Nations championship was on the cards for the first time for nine years. All told, 15 full international matches were due to be played that winter.

The outbreak of war on the first weekend of the season meant goodbye to all that. On arrival, the Australian tourists spent a week on the south coast packing sand-bags before joining up, while the Home Unions promptly cancelled all fixtures for the season. Clubs were eventually permitted to arrange games if they were prepared to comply with government war-time regulations and an interesting informal season followed while Britain waited uneasily during a period of Phoney War.

However, an Army XV full of international players took part in a highly entertaining match at the Parc des Princes against France in February of that season. The French, delighted at their return to international competition, awarded full international caps to their players. By doing so they made the match unique in the game's history, for it stands as the only major official international ever staged on a continent at war.

The Army XV, which defeated the French 36–3, was a high-powered side. Its players read like a cavalcade of British Rugby stars of the 1930s: Viv Jenkins, Peter Cranmer, Wilf Wooller, Sammy Walker, Mike Sayers, Blair Mayne and Bill Travers. All were among the top players of their generation and most of them had toured South Africa with Walker's 1938 Lions. Many reckoned the team to be one of the best British sides ever. Wooller was outstanding, scoring a hat trick of spectacular tries and Jenkins kicked seven conversions.

The only other major Test staged during wartime was in August 1914 when the All Blacks and Wallabies played the third international of a New Zealand tour to Australia. The match in Sydney took place shortly after the Great War broke out in Europe.

END OF THE ROAD

TEDDINGTON, JANUARY 1945

Which was the most successful club side ever? It's an impossible question to answer but nonetheless one that is debated endlessly in any number of pubs and clubs. The Oxford University side of the 1880s enjoyed a long unbeaten run in the early days of the game, and Harlequins enjoyed a successful spell in the years leading up to the outbreak of the Great War at about the same time as they moved to Twickenham.

Then there were the Northampton teams of the 1950s, who for more than a decade had at least one representative in every England Test side, while in the more recent era of the Cup and Leagues, Bath's records take some beating. But the common ground shared by such successful sides is that, whenever they were beaten, there was always genuine surprise among the spectators that the favourites had been overcome.

The end of what must be the longest run of victories by a club side was witnessed by a similarly dumbfounded crowd at Teddington in January 1945 when a young St Mary's Hospital XV, with an exciting midfield triangle, brought to an end the golden run of Coventry in a tense match. It was the medics' Nim Hall, later a distinguished utility back for England, who was the architect of the home side's win. The fly half dropped both of his side's goals (worth four points apiece then) in an 8–3 win against the Midlanders.

The result marked the end of a truly incredible run of 72 victories by the Coventry club which dated back to December

1941. In that time they had amassed 1712 points and conceded only 254. That they should lose to a team of student doctors added to the surprise of the thousand or so spectators who were present at the match. For the record, Coventry beat the medics 14–0 in a return match at Coundon Road a couple of weeks later.

PASSPORT SCAM

PARIS, APRIL 1946

After the wartime break, responsibility for arranging inter-national matches returned to the Home Unions in 1945 and for the season 1945–6 an informal series of representative matches was staged. Additional interest was provided by the Kiwis, a team of New Zealand Services players who engaged in inter-nationals with England, Scotland, Wales and France, although no caps were awarded by the British or Irish unions. With many British servicemen still abroad, it was argued by the Home Unions that their international sides were not truly repre-sentative. The French, however, recognised all of their matches as full cap games.

The public, untroubled by the issue of caps or not, flocked in their thousands to see a series of matches that became known as the 'Victory Internationals'. There was no championship at stake, because it was impossible to arrange a complete round-robin of fixtures but this did not detract from the allure of the fixtures.

The last international of the series was staged at Stade Colombes where Wales were the visitors but, due to last minute changes, the party travelling to Paris for the match had to deceive Customs in order to field a full fifteen.

Cliff Davies, the Kenfig Hill miner who was one of the most popular Welsh players of his generation, was supposed to prop for Wales on this occasion. When he was injured in a colliery accident shortly before the party was due to set off for France, his cousin, Billy Jones, was hurriedly drafted into the side despite suffering a painful ear injury playing for Cardiff against the Barbarians on the eve of departure.

There was, however, a problem. Billy Jones had never been abroad and didn't possess a passport. Fortunately, for the Welsh party, he bore a strong resemblance to his cousin and this presented a way round the problem. Billy simply travelled under Cliff Davies's name and carried his cousin's papers. And he got away with it. All the match reports of the game reported the name C Davies (Cardiff) in the team line-ups for the game. One critic at the match even referred to 'Cliff Davies's fine play', which must have tickled the two cousins pink.

Whether the Welsh Rugby Union enlightened the press and asked for confidentiality about the change is unknown, but certainly everyone in the cousins' home village of Kenfig Hill, where both of them were local heroes, knew the secret of the Welsh front-row in that last international of the 'Victory' season.

For the record, France won by 12–0, their halves successfully blotting out the threat posed by the Cardiff pair of Billy Cleaver and Haydn Tanner.

THE ALL BLACK DAY

WELLINGTON & DURBAN, SEPTEMBER 1949

Saturday 3 September, 1949 was a unique day in the history of international rugby. For the only time since Tests began in March 1871, a country fielded two separate fifteens on the same day for cap matches.

The country in question was New Zealand and the games took place on two different continents. The day began in Wellington where virtually the third New Zealand XV faced Australia in the opening match of a two-match series. The Wallabies, led by Trevor Allan, played effective rugby and scored three tries in the 20 minutes leading up to the interval to lead 11–0.

New Zealand came back after the break. Jack Kelly landed an eighth minute penalty before Graham Moore, on his only appearance in an All Black shirt, scored a try. But Australia's determined defence held up and at full time the score was 11–6 to the Wallabies, who thus registered their first success against New Zealand for 15 years.

Later the same day, across the Indian Ocean in South Africa where New Zealand's leading thirty players were simultaneously making a major tour, the All Blacks played the third match of their Test series in Durban. They had already lost the first two matches of the series and for this game their tour skipper, Fred Allen, had been dropped. Bad enough as these events were for New Zealand rugby fans, for those who listened in late at night to the radio commentary of the events of that match there was even more depressing news to swallow. After a promising first half the tourists eventually went down 9–3, thus losing their third consecutive Test in South Africa and with it the chance of squaring the series.

This sequence of losing Test matches was extended to six by the end of the 1949 season as New Zealand went on to lose the Fourth Test in South Africa and the second Test against Australia. Never before and never since have the All Blacks lost six Tests on the trot and, if 1949 has gone down in their rugby annals as the Black Year, then Saturday 3 September 1949 was certainly their Black Day.

ARMY FORGETS ITS DRILL

TWICKENHAM, APRIL 1950

During the 1950 season, the Army were the unbeaten winners of the annual Inter-Services Triangular tournament and went into the traditional annual match against their French counterparts on All Fools' Day as hot favourites to continue their successful run.

For once, though, the Army forgot its drill in an extraordinary start to the match. As the home side was warming up to go out onto the Twickenham pitch their experienced full-back, Lieut. Roberts, tweaked a leg muscle and had to withdraw from the XV. Normally, one of the reserves would have stepped in, but the Army's reserve players had already left the dressing rooms and were making their way to seats high in the West Stand.

No contingency plan was in place and there was nothing for it but for the Army to start the match with only 14 players. Chaos ruled for the next 20 minutes as desperate messages were relayed over the loudspeaker system urging one of the reserves to return to the changing rooms and get stripped to join the action on the field. At length, Captain Scarr of the Hussars emerged to complete the team.

By then fully 25 minutes had passed and the French Army had taken advantage of the situation, taking a six-point lead and playing with their tails up. Although the British Army, fielding six seasoned internationals and playing with the stiff breeze after the interval, did give their opponents a stern test in the second half, the result was a well merited 12–8 win for a visiting side that contained only one international player.

No doubt the Army rugby authorities absorbed the moral of this episode in subsequent seasons: keep your reserves where you know that you can lay your hands on them.

FATHER VERSUS SON

GISBORNE, SEPTEMBER 1950

The first time that a father and son faced one another in a first-class match in New Zealand was in September 1950. George Nepia senior, golden boy of the 1924–5 Invincible Second All Blacks who toured Britain and France, was 45 years of age when he turned out at full-back for the Olympians invitation club against Poverty Bay in Gisborne.

Opposite him, also as full-back, was his son, George Nepia junior. Both players were captains of their sides on a day when age triumphed over youth. The Olympians won 17–11, the victorious captain setting another record on that occasion by becoming the oldest New Zealander to feature in a first-class match.

MURRAYFIELD MASSACRE

EDINBURGH, FEBRUARY 1951

Scotland won a rare and famous victory that is still discussed when old men gather to talk about the Five Nations championship. Wales, the reigning Grand Slam champions, started their match against virtual no-hopers, Scotland, at a cracking pace in front of a then world record attendance of 80,000 spectators, nearly a quarter of whom were Welsh. They tore into the Scots and immediately put them on the defensive.

Twelve of the Welsh XV had toured Australia and New Zealand with the Lions several months earlier, but Scotland showed that they were no great respecters of reputations and safely survived the initial Welsh onslaught. Scotland's loose trio effectively disrupted the Welsh halves and fly-half Glyn Davies was so harassed out of the game that towards the end of the match the Welsh captain, John Gwilliam, in desperation rearranged his midfield and switched Lewis Jones from centre to the pivot position.

The Scottish back row in fact had set the agenda almost from the start of the match. At the first scrum, Wales heeled the ball and Rex Willis threw out a routine pass to Davies, his half-back partner. The Scottish flankers, Doug Elliot and Bob Taylor, were on him like hawks and poor Davies was buried beneath a wave of marauding blue jerseys. Aggressive defence was to be the key to Scotland's growing threat. As the first half progressed, Scotland gained the upper hand up front and it hardly surprised the experts when the Scots reached half time nursing a slender 3–0 lead, their full-back Ian Thomson having kicked a penalty goal.

134

The third quarter of the match was uneventful until Peter Kininmonth, the Scottish captain, inspired his side with an unexpected score. Welsh full-back Gerwyn Williams missed touch with a kick from inside his own 25. Kininmonth caught the ball near the touchline, lined the goal up in his sights and sent a lovely drop goal spiralling between the posts.

Thereafter the Scottish backs played sound rugby football to score three tries against a Welsh defence that fell to pieces. New cap Robert Gordon crossed twice, supporting a break by Donald Scott for the first try and diving on a loose ball after a rush led by Doug Elliot for his second. Jim Dawson, a forward, completed the rout of the Welshmen, scoring seconds from time when he picked up in the loose and charged over.

Scotland's famous massacre of Wales – wins by 19–0 were very rare in the early post war era – stands as the most remarkable 'David and Goliath' match in Five Nations history. 'This was one of the most extraordinary results I can remember,' began Dai Gent in his *Sunday Times* report of the match. Gent, never one to overstate the case, had played international rugby as far back as 1905 and, in a long and distinguished career in journalism, was one of the game's most knowledgeable and respected critics.

Many explanations were offered for what amounted to an incredible change in Welsh form: the more plausible were that too many of their players were stale after the long Lions tour and that the team were complacent after giving England a 23–5 hiding only a fortnight earlier.

Yet the truth of the matter was that Scotland were the more enthusiastic side and wanted the win more than the Welsh did. The spirited Scots thoroughly deserved their great triumph but, had they known what lay in store for them, they would gladly have settled for a less spectacular win in return for more victories.

For before the year was out the Scots were involved in another Murrayfield massacre when they were on the receiving end of a 44–0 thrashing by the touring Springboks. And four more years (and 17 successive Tests) would pass before Scotland again won an international match.

DID THE TOUCH JUDGE HELP WALES?

CARDIFF, DECEMBER 1953

Until 1963 Wales had never lost to the All Blacks at Cardiff. It is incredible to reflect today that their wins there in 1905, 1935 and 1953 once gave them a 3–1 lead in this series (they lost at Swansea in 1924). Even so, there was never more than one score between the sides in the matches won by Wales.

Probably the luckiest Welsh win of the three was in 1953 when they beat New Zealand for the last time. It was 8–5 to New Zealand as the game entered its last quarter. Welsh threequarter Gareth Griffiths had gone off the field with a badly dislocated shoulder in the first half, but pleaded with the Welsh Rugby Union's surgeon, Nathan Rocyn Jones, to allow him to return to the match. Griffiths was very persuasive and, soon after he returned, Wales redoubled their efforts and managed to kick a penalty goal that levelled the scores. Five minutes from time Griffiths was to figure in the move that led to the winning score of the match.

He and left wing Gwyn Rowlands put pressure on New Zealand's Allan Elsom, some 20 yards from the All Blacks line. As the ball went loose, Clem Thomas picked it up and, finding himself cornered close to the touchline, cross kicked. The ball bounced into the path of the Welsh right wing, Ken Jones, who raced over for a try at the posts which Rowlands converted. 13–8 to Wales and that was that.

It was another Welsh winner against New Zealand, Viv Jenkins of the 1935 side, who later spun an intriguing tale around that winning move. He became a leading post-war rugby journalist, first with the *News of the World* and later for the *Sunday Times*. Jenkins attended the dinner after the 1953 match and was seated beside another former Welsh great, Ifor Jones of Llanelli, who regularly acted as Wales's touch judge during the 1950s. Jones had been running the line that afternoon.

Discussing the day's game, Ifor Jones divulged to Jenkins that at the instant Clem Thomas picked the ball up, he had yelled, 'Cross-kick, Clem; Ken Jones is unmarked.' Did a touch judge really help Wales to beat the All Blacks?

Although referees were neutral of course, those were the days when each of the sides playing provided their own touch judge for international matches. Usually these were members of the participating Unions' committees or distinguished referees. More than 30 years were to pass before neutral touch judges arrived on the international match scene.

Ifor Jones and Clem Thomas, sadly both dead now, were great characters and wonderful story tellers. The truth of the tale has never been proved. But certainly the film of that winning move shows the Welsh touch judge right up with the play at the time of Thomas's cross-kick. Ifor Jones was unquestionably in the ideal position to influence the kicker. Clem Thomas, moreover, was described as looking pale and worried during the match, weighed down no doubt by the distress of having been involved in a fatal road accident on his journey down to Cardiff on the eve of the game.

It is easy to believe that Clem was operating on auto-pilot for once in a distinguished rugby career that culminated in his captaincy of Wales in nine matches in 1958 and 1959, and that he was quite happy to follow the inspired instructions of 'his' touch judge. But many of Clem's friends on hearing this story years later insisted that the tale was more likely to be the product of Ifor Jones's fertile imagination.

Clem was a well-known rugby journalist up to the time of his death. His former Press Box colleagues, all of whom retain the fondest memories of him, categorically dismiss the story: 'Can't be true', they say almost to a man. 'Clem would never have done as he was told.'

THE OVERBEARING CAPTAIN

TWICKENHAM, FEBRUARY 1955

Jean Prat was the outstanding French rugby player of his generation. He was a regular fixture in the Tricolores' XV from 1945 until his retirement from internationals in 1955 and did much to raise the profile of French club rugby in immediate post-war seasons. At his own beloved Lourdes he fittingly performed miracles, raising the small town club to champions of France.

Determination and tenacity, legacies of his prowess as a long-distance runner, were the distinguishing features of his own game and when, in 1953, the captaincy of the French side fell vacant he was seen as the natural choice to lead the side. Within twelve months he had taken France to the top of the Five Nations Championship for their first ever title.

He had at his disposal a very young side in 1954 and led with an iron fist. Instigating a tight-marking policy he carried his men to wins against Scotland, Ireland, New Zealand and England, though a narrow defeat against Wales in Cardiff meant that France's maiden Five Nations title had to be shared.

The 1955 season, he had decided, would be his last in international colours and Monsieur Rugby, as he was called on both sides of the Channel, decided that he wanted an all-out commitment from a team that he was determined to lead to the Grand Slam. Wins against Scotland and Ireland took his unbeaten men to a difficult contest with England at Twickenham on the last Saturday of February.

The match at rugby's Mecca was a tight one and Prat gave one of his best individual performances. He so dominated the proceedings that even his own team were in awe of him. Amédée Domenech, then a callow prop, found his captain's exhortations to do this, do that and do everything so over-bearing that at one point, finding himself unexpectedly in possession, he determined to put his captain in a likewise situation. He passed the ball like a hot potato to Prat. But before Domenech could mutter, 'Here, see what you can do with it,' the captain had dropped his second goal of the match and set his side on course for a 16–9 win – only their second success since 1911 at Twickenham. Domenech was dumb-founded.

LAST MINUTE MISS

JOHANNESBURG, AUGUST 1955

They called this the greatest Test of all time. The Lions were on their first post-war tour of South Africa and entered the opening Test of the four-match series with a string of good results to their name. Playing behind a fit and mobile pack, the Lions' backs had performed brilliantly in the provincial matches leading up to the Test and, with Wales's Cliff Morgan to marshal the threequarters, the side was encouraged to take its provincial form and approach into the internationals.

Morgan had at his disposal a division that was a devastating mix of attacking genius and dependable defence. Jeff Butterfield and Phil Davies of England were an effective pair of centres who delivered a continuous supply of scoring opportunities to the young Irish teenager, Tony O'Reilly, on the wing. In the pack, the all-Welsh front row of Courtenay Meredith, Billy Williams and Bryn Meredith were sterling scrummagers while behind them, Rhys Williams and Scotland's Jim Greenwood brought strength and all-round skills in the tight and loose.

The tourists' reputation for quality rugby attracted a new world record of 95,000 spectators to Ellis Park for the Test. The kilted Ernie Michie, one of the Lions reserve locks, led the tourists on to the pitch accompanied by the skirl of his bagpipes, but the first half went in favour of South Africa who led 11–8 at the interval. The first period was a heady see-saw affair but the events of the second half raised the game to an even higher plane.

140

The Lions galvanised themselves to play flowing rugby for a purple patch early in the third quarter. Loose forward Reg Higgins had retired with a knee injury as soon as the second half had started, but Cliff Morgan set the scoreboard rolling when he broke from a scrum inside the South African 25 to arc round for a classic fly-half try under the posts. Angus Cameron converted and in the space of eight minutes converted further tries by Jim Greenwood and Tony O'Reilly to take the Lions up to 23–11.

Surely the Lions could not lose now, despite having to struggle with only seven forwards? Sias Swart squeezed in at the left corner to pull back three points for South Africa with a try, but, even when Jack van der Schyff converted a try by Chris Koch on the stroke of time, the small band of British followers in the crowd felt that they were home and dry.

But more drama was to come. In the third minute of injury time Theunis Briers just evaded Jeff Butterfield's tackle to score to the right of the posts, leaving van der Schyff with a kick that could give the Springboks a 24–23 victory. The full-back, who had been a model of consistency throughout the match, prepared to take the last kick of the match. Standing two-thirds of the way between goal and corner flag, van der Schyff carried the hopes of all South Africa. Surely the man they called the automaton in deference to his immaculate kicking style would deliver?

He steadied himself, ran up to take his kick but sent the ball wide. It was the bitterest moment of the match and a picture taken of the poor full-back immediately after his moment of failure perfectly conveys his mood of utter dejection. He is shown with his head bowed and fingers stretched like a convicted man tensing himself for the moment that the trapdoor opens on the gallows. The most exciting match for years had ended in a one-point win for the Lions.

The 1955 tour was the first to receive widespread media coverage. Film sent back to Britain was eagerly awaited by a British sporting public whose imaginations had been captured by the success of the tourists, while Viv Jenkins (*Sunday Times*) and Bryn Thomas (*Western Mail*) became the first British journalists to report a Lions tour. Thomas had no doubt that this was among the greatest struggles that he had witnessed. 'From the first whistle to the last the match produced an atmosphere of intense excitement with swift moving play of exceptionally high standard. Such a match comes but once in a generation,' he told his readers on the Monday following this famous win.

ENTIRE WELSH XV ORDERED OFF

CARDIFF, MARCH 1957

International matches at Cardiff in the late 1950s and early 1960s were invariably mud-baths. The history of the ground until its redevelopment as the National Stadium in 1969 was closely associated with famous Welsh matches played on what one critic described as far back as the 1920s as their own 'primordial slime'.

Many people will have fond memories of being drenched on the old, open East or West terraces at the Arms Park. In March 1957, Wales hosted Ireland on a typical South Wales day. The rain had been falling in stair-rods from a slate grey sky since dawn when the sides squelched their way across the turf and lined up for the start of a match that odds-on would depend on weight advantage.

But on this occasion the conditions were so bad that the referee was prompted to take action that was subsequently outlawed by the game's rule makers, the International Board.

Wales took the lead after eight minutes when Terry Davies kicked a penalty goal from a wide angle after Ireland had infringed at a line-out. The ball was still relatively new and light at this stage, which could not be said ten minutes later when Ireland missed the first of three attempts to equalise from positions that would have been considered easy in different weather.

Passing and running were becoming increasingly difficult as the pitch turned into a quagmire and it was to their considerable credit that Ireland managed to fashion a try mid-

143

way through the first half. The conditions were entirely to blame for a Welsh lapse.

Cliff Morgan was caught in possession and sent a pass backwards to Terry Davies, his full-back. Davies lost his footing and as he fell the slippery ball spilled loose, whereupon back-row forward Ronnie Kavanagh dived on it to claim a try that, from close range, Cecil Pedlow converted to give Ireland the lead.

Play in the second half became a lottery. The heavier Welsh forwards, however, began to take charge of the set-pieces, though no-one looked capable in the difficult conditions of holding the ball long enough to create a try.

On the hour the referee blew loudly on his whistle and began talking earnestly to both captains. At length the entire Welsh XV left the field with the apparent blessing of the referee. The thirty players had become so camouflaged by the mud that it had become impossible for the official to tell the teams apart, so he had offered both teams the opportunity of changing into clean shirts.

Only the Welsh took up his offer. The Irish preferred to stay on the field in the wet and cold, running on the spot while the Welsh retreated to the warm, dry dressing rooms. Undoubtedly Ireland erred in their decision. For when the Welsh returned they were noticeably uplifted by the change of kit and ten minutes later forced a penalty from which Terry Davies, at point blank range, was able to lift the heavy ball over the crossbar for the winning points.

The referee making his international debut on this occasion was the Scottish official, Jack Taylor. A former Leicester fly-half, Jack was for many years a master at the famous Scottish school, Loretto. His unusual action in offering the teams the chance to go off was not appreciated by the International Board. He was not invited to officiate at an international match for three years and when the game's law books were amended for the 1957–58 season, a clause prohibiting teams to leave the field at any time between kick-off and no-side was inserted.

Mr Taylor did eventually return to Wales on international duty in 1960 for the Wales v South Africa clash. Unfortunately for him the conditions then were even worse than they had been for the Irish match. (The morning after the South Africa clash the river Taff burst its banks and flooded the Arms Park). During the match the pitch turned into such a morass that the touch- and goal-lines became completely obliterated. There were also frequent stoppages while players had to use towels to remove mud from their eyes.

Unable to interrupt the match this time, either for the players to change or for the groundsman to re-paint the markings, Mr Taylor simply offered to abandon the game after 55 minutes. But his offer was turned down. Terry Davies, Wales's captain, steadfastly refused, believing that his side could win as they were trailing by only three points and had the gale behind their backs. South Africa, however, somehow managed to hold on to win in conditions to which they were 'loathsomely unaccustomed'.

Certainly, Jack Taylor never forgot his refereeing experiences at Cardiff.

THREE REFEREES FOR ONE MATCH

PAHIATUA, SEPTEMBER 1957

The game between Bush and Wanganui played at Rugby Park, Pahiatua, near the end of the New Zealand domestic season in 1957 was unique for the fact that three referees were used in a first-class match.

The official who started the game was Roy Rice. He was then injured in a collision with a player scoring a try and had to withdraw to the touchline for treatment. As preparations for the conversion kick were being made, Leith Parker, one of the match-day touch-judges who was also the president of the Bush Union, stepped in to supervise the kick and awarded the points for the successful conversion.

When it became apparent that Mr Rice would be unable to complete the match, a third referee, Wray Hewitt, officiated for the rest of the game with Leith Parker returning to the touchline. Bush ran out 20–16 winners of this their last home fixture of the season.

A CAP BEFORE A JERSEY

TWICKENHAM, JANUARY 1958

One of the biggest moments of a Welsh international rugby player's career is when he changes for his first appearance and slips the red jersey over his head. The years of waiting, dreaming and toiling for recognition finally come to an end as the realisation that he is finally about to represent his country sinks in. A quick glance down to the heart region of the coveted shirt and there are the three feathers, the proud insignia of the ancient Princes of Wales – an emblem that distinguishes it from the ordinary garb of a red club jersey and instils great pride in the wearer.

There was no such moment, however, for Haydn Morgan, the red-headed Abertillery open-side forward when he pulled on his first Welsh jersey in the Twickenham dressing rooms in January 1958. Not that he didn't have any pride – far from it. But on looking down at his shirt, the only new cap in a fifteen captained by Cliff Morgan, he discovered that the Welsh badge was missing.

He wasn't alone. The whole side had jerseys that were without badges. In effect, they were trial jerseys. As former Wales outside-half, Cliff Jones, one of the 1958 selection committee explained, 'It couldn't be helped, the makers sent us the wrong kit and the mistake wasn't discovered until it was opened in the dressing rooms.'

Haydn Morgan thus became unique among the nine hundred-plus players who have turned out for Wales: he was awarded his international cap before he had played in a proper Welsh jersey.

147

Wales had played in trial jerseys under similar circumstances in Belfast almost fifty years earlier. But on this occasion there were no new caps – every member of the Welsh XV had already played for Wales.

WHERE'S OUR CROSS-BAR?

TWICKENHAM, JANUARY 1958

That same England-Wales game at Twickenham in January 1958 is remembered in West Wales for a very different reason. During the match the Welsh full-back, Terry Davies, very nearly landed a winning penalty goal with a colossal kick from 50 yards into a swirling wind. His attempt missed, veering into the posts at the last minute and the match ended in a 3–3 draw. But the miss prompted a most peculiar incident during the weekend.

Later that evening in central London, a plan was hatched by a young Welsh supporter. Aided and abetted by the brother of his fiancée, who lived in nearby Ealing, the Welshman returned to Twickenham during the early hours of Sunday morning, climbed over the turnstiles and proceeded to saw down the cross-bar from the offending posts at the north end of the ground. In a 20-minute operation the bar was cut into three lengths before it was whisked away down the A40 back to West Wales later in the day.

On his way home the phantom woodworker from south Pembrokeshire stopped in a Cotswold café for some refreshment. By coincidence, Terry Davies had also pulled in to the same café while motoring back to his home in Bynea outside Llanelli. The prankster promptly told Terry the story and persuaded him to autograph the mementoes.

The then secretary of the Rugby Football Union (RFU) was Col Frank Prentice who broke the news of the incident to the press on the Monday morning. Taking the loss in a sporting manner he added that the RFU had made arrangements to replace the bar. It was at that stage that Terry Davies intervened. Davies, as it happened, was a timber merchant and offered to replace the cross-bar.

'If it will save the lad any trouble,' he told the *Western Mail*, 'I would be glad to replace the bar. I am sure many people in Wales would like to know who the joker was. But I hope cross-bars are not going to keep vanishing after international matches and that I shall not be expected to continue replacing them. That could lead to bankruptcy.'

At length, the joker and his conspirators' consciences got the better of them. They had thought that their prank would have been quickly forgotten, but such an incident had never occurred at Twickenham before and when the respected Welsh critic and rugby writer, Bryn Thomas, advised them to write a letter of apology to the RFU, they decided to make a clean breast of the matter. A couple of days after the joke they decided to write to Col Prentice.

The perpetrators of this good humoured prank were revealed as Fred Mathias, the Welsh champion jockey from Manorbier in Pembrokeshire, and his bride-to-be's brother, Brian Attewell of Ealing. Thus blame was shared by an Englishman and a Welshman and fortunately there the matter ended.

To this day, one of the autographed pieces of cross-bar has pride of place in Mathias's local pub in Pembrokeshire.

TWICKENHAM LOSES ITS DECORUM

TWICKENHAM, FEBRUARY 1958

The Fourth Wallabies who toured Britain, Ireland and France in 1957–8 are remembered as a curious Jekyll and Hyde party. Off the field, they were pleasant, personable young men who made friends wherever they went. But their methods on the field were often questioned, accusations of over vigorous play being levelled against them from as early as the third match of the visit – an unexpected defeat at the hands of a young Cambridge University side.

The tourists were also dogged by injuries, the most serious of which was to Jim Phipps, their first-choice centre who broke his leg. It meant that the teenager, Jim Lenehan, who was originally selected as understudy to Terry Curley at full-back, had to be used as a first choice centre for the majority of the tour.

Lenehan was a prodigious left-footed kicker and a devastating tackler and it was one of his tackles in the match at Swansea that nearly sparked off a riot. He crashed into the little Swansea fly-half, Bryan Richards, with a late tackle in the second half that incensed the local crowd. There were catcalls and boos every time Lenehan received the ball after that, and many flare-ups among the players led to flying fists and misplaced boots. The wonder of it all was that nobody was sent off.

Lenehan was again the centre of controversy when the Wallabies played against England at Twickenham. The crowds

151

at Headquarters have always had a reputation for enjoying their champagne parties in the car park before behaving sedately during even the roughest of matches. But for the first time Twickenham lost its decorum when the young Australian slid knees-first into England left wing, Peter Thompson, who had already been flattened by a tackle. This incident took place early on in the match at the south-east corner of the ground and it so roused the crowd that they, like the spectators at Swansea, subsequently booed Lenehan every time he became involved in the match.

This unprecedented behaviour by the crowd marred the match according to the press. The booing was 'of an ugliness even old campaigners could not recall previously at Twickenham,' reported Denys Rowbotham for the *Guardian*.

As the game developed, more and more of England's backs were in the wars. Jeff Butterfield was three times late tackled, Phil Horrocks-Taylor was off for an hour with a calf injury, Jim Hetherington was concussed and Dickie Jeeps bruised his right hand. Only Malcolm Phillips in the centre escaped lasting injury.

Fortunately at the end of the match there was one of those sporting moments when time stands still and every pulse quickens. In the dying minutes, the crocked England back division managed to ship the ball out to the right wing where Peter Jackson gathered on the Australian 25. Swerving past defenders and handing off would-be tacklers he beat a path for the corner where he leapt with a do-or-die dive for the winning try. The crowd erupted with joy, quickly forgetting the ugly scenes of the previous hour. In their jubilation they perhaps felt vindicated.

The match, always remembered for the Jackson try, nevertheless shocked the sporting fraternity. Even the well-known *Daily Express* cartoonist, Roy Ullyett, ended his strip with a record of the day that 'the Twickenham crowd went all common and booed'.

PLEASE CAN WE HAVE OUR BALL BACK?

COVENTRY, FEBRUARY 1958

The last match played by the Fourth Wallabies in England was against the Midland Counties at Highfield Road, the ground of Coventry City football club. The match play was not particularly distinguished, although the home side, comprising 13 Warwickshire players, did achieve its first win over a touring team for 30 years.

The bare playing surface, which in wet conditions churned into a mud-bath, did not ease the running and handling for the backs of either side, though both fifteens did attempt to play open rugby. Coventry scrum-half George Cole put the Midlands ahead with a left-footed penalty goal after 20 minutes and Ron Harvey equalised early in the second half with a similar score for the Wallabies.

Fenwick Allison, an England full-back and the home side's captain, won the match ten minutes later when he was up in support of a threequarter move and took an inside pass from wing Peter Jackson to score wide out. Cole converted to conclude the scoring: an 8–3 win for the Midlands.

If the play was forgettable, one moment stood out. A hugely entertaining episode of farce made this match a memorable one for the 10,000 who saw it. George Cole and Fenwick Allison on the home side together with Jim Lenehan and Terry Curley in the Australian XV were four of the most prodigious out-of-the-hand kickers of a rugby ball playing in the late 1950s. Twice during the early stages of the game match balls were kicked on to the top of the Highfield Road stands where they remained.

But when Allison had lodged a third ball on top of the roof, play ground to a complete standstill. Only three balls had been provided for the game and, this being a football ground, there were no spare or practice rugby balls lying around anywhere.

Allison himself, together with a couple of policemen, made earnest enquiries as the crowd became restless at the lack of action on the pitch. Eventually the long-suffering spectators were provided with the best entertainment of the afternoon. There was no alternative but for the groundstaff to march on to the pitch with an enormous ladder and clamber up to the roof. This brought light relief to the crowd, who burst into laughter and began clapping as a full-scale operation to recover the balls began.

While the intrepid groundsman spent five minutes recovering three rugby balls from the roof, a spectator tossed a souvenir miniature one on to the field, where it was enthusiastically received by the Australians who proceeded to further amuse the crowd with a mock game.

FRENCH TURN ON THEIR SELECTORS

PARIS, MARCH 1958

One of the most embarrassing crowd disturbances at an international match took place in March 1958 at the Stade Colombes stadium in Paris, scene of the 1924 Olympics. French rugby had made great strides in the Five Nations championship in the post-war years. Their first win on Welsh soil (1948), first at Twickenham (1951) and first at Murrayfield (1952) were followed by Five Nations shared titles in both 1954 and 1955. The sport was enjoying a growing following among the French public and hopes were high that a Five Nations outright title would soon be theirs.

Then progress went pear-shaped. France were whitewashed in the 1957 championship and lost their opening Five Nations match of 1958 to Scotland. Their next opponents were England and, with a maiden tour of South Africa to come in the summer, it was imperative that the national side should start to string together some significant Test wins.

The England match in Paris was to prove a watershed in French fortunes. More than 60,000 spectators arrived to see France capitulate after 20 minutes. Peter Thompson opened England's account with a try from a kick ahead by Ricky Bartlett and his second try, five minutes later, sparked off a near riot. In an unprecedented move, the crowd turned on Monsieur Roger Lerou, the chairman of the French selectors who was seated in the stand. They yelled obscenities at him and the rest of his selection committee. 'Démission, démission

155

(resign, resign)', was the most polite expression of the crowd's discontent. Only the strategic positioning of the French police prevented the demonstration from turning violent.

A thoroughly dispirited French side caved in completely after the interval and crashed to their sixth successive Five Nations reverse and their heaviest defeat by England since before the Great War. But it's a long road that has no winding. That remarkable crowd demonstration shook the French selectors to their bones. Wholesale changes behind the scrum were made for their next international against Australia the following week. But this was too late to prevent the French crowd voting with their feet – less than 30,000 were present to witness an extraordinary change in fortunes. The French defeated Australia 19–0. They then went on to defeat Wales in Cardiff for the first time and returned from South Africa a couple of months later as the first country to take a home Test series off the Springboks since 1903.

Talk about a demonstration having its desired effect! France won the Five Nations title outright in 1959 and their championship results relative to the Home Unions for the decade between that England match in 1958 and the corresponding fixture in 1968 speak for themselves.

	P	W	D	L	%
France	40	26	6	8	72.5
Wales	40	19	5	16	53.8
England	40	13	12	15	47.5
Scotland	40	15	5	20	43.8
Ireland	40	11	4	25	32.5

SEVEN SHIRT CHANGES

SWANSEA, APRIL 1958

For the greater part of the twentieth century the curtain came down on the representative season in Britain with the traditional Barbarians' Easter visit to South Wales. In its heyday the tour comprised four matches: Penarth on Good Friday, Cardiff on Easter Saturday, and Swansea and Newport on Easter Monday and Tuesday respectively.

The match at Swansea in April 1958 was described as the most ragged in Barbarians' history. Not because it was a scrappy game that did not come alive until the final ten minutes, but because of the numerous stoppages for shirt changes. All told, seven Barbarian shirts had to be replaced with Gordon Waddell, their young Scotland fly-half, having three jerseys ripped off his back.

The Scot shook off the rough-housing in the second half and brought a dreary match to the boil with a 30-yard run through a forest of defenders to send Welsh lock Roddy Evans over for a try. Arthur Smith had kicked an earlier penalty.

The Barbarians were thus 6–0 ahead as the game moved into injury and jersey-changing time at the end. Swansea scored during the extra time when centre Gordon Lewis ripped through a gap to send flanker Ron Lloyd, a gentleman of the cloth who had been described as a fine example of muscular Christianity, in for a try that Dai Parkhouse converted. Final score: Swansea 5, Barbarians 6, Torn jerseys 7.

FRANCE CLAIM WORLD CROWN

JOHANNESBURG, AUGUST 1958

The path-finding French tour of South Africa in 1958 received little coverage in the British newspapers, yet it was one of the most significant events in the history of international rugby. For a start, it was the first short tour by a northern hemisphere union to the south. But the surprise outcome was that South Africa lost a home series for the first time since 1896, the victory by the French in the second Test announcing their arrival as a major force in world rugby.

The tour included ten matches, two of which were internationals, but the Test series caught South African rugby in confusion. The Springboks had ruled the roost of world rugby, home and away, from 1896 until sharing the series with the Lions in 1955. This was then followed by a disappointing tour of New Zealand in 1956 when the 'Boks' lost their first ever Test series to the All Blacks. When the French arrived, South African rugby was at a cross-roads, suffering in particular from a dearth of attacking half-backs. Even so, any thoughts of losing to the French were simply not entertained: South Africans did not lose Test rugby series on their own soil, especially against the French who were regarded on the veldt as the Cinderellas of world rugby.

As it turned out, the result of the series underlined South Africa's drop from its high estate. In the first Test in Cape Town, South Africa's makeshift fly-half, Ian Kirkpatrick, adopted dour tactics. Time and again good possession went to waste through unimaginative kicking and the French were pleased to draw a match that they could even have won.

For the second Test, the South African selectors made seven changes and one positional adjustment. Although they led by a converted try to a penalty goal at half time, the Springboks were outplayed in the set-pieces after the interval and a couple of dropped goals carried France to the most unexpected series win of the century.

News of the French success took precedence over all other sports news on Radio France and in the French press. 'Most sensational victory in the history of French rugby,' was the lead story in Paris's *Dimanche Soir*. 'France become world champions,' announced *Paris Presse* on its front page.

And to think, France had never even won the Five Nations outright before this tour. The South African adventure certainly stimulated interest in rugby throughout France and in the season that followed the French carried off the International Championship title for the first time. They were to remain European champions for four seasons.

GAME THAT STARTED A DEBATE

DUNEDIN, JULY 1959

Ever since Billy Bancroft landed the first one in an international in 1893, the penalty goal was referred to as the game's illegitimate child. By the 1950s more and more big matches were being decided by penalty goals, prompting a growing number of rugby's administrators, not to mention press critics, to campaign for a change to the laws of the game.

It was against this background that the Lions set off for New Zealand to meet the All Blacks in a four-match Test series in 1959. New Zealand had uncovered a prodigious place kicker in Don Clarke three years earlier. The Don had come into their side midway through an exciting series against the Springboks, and his place kicking had played a significant part in New Zealand's subsequent Test series win, their first ever against South Africa.

Clarke was the world's number one goal kicker when the 1959 series opened and the visiting Lions knew that he, more than any other New Zealander, was the biggest threat to their winning the series. They weren't wrong.

For the first Test, the Lions selected a back division that had all the talents. Ken Scotland was the best attacking full back in the four Home Unions, Peter Jackson and Tony O'Reilly on the wings would have been the automatic choices for any World XV of the day and Dickie Jeeps, the india-rubber man at scrum-half, was the most courageous half back in the game. They thrilled New Zealand crowds with their panoply of skills on that tour and were prominent in giving the Lions a 9–6 half time lead in the Test played on the Carisbrook ground at Dunedin.

The Lions started the second half positively and in the next 25 minutes added tries by Peter Jackson and Welsh centre, Malcolm Price. In between, Don Clarke had kicked the All Blacks' third penalty goal so that, with a quarter of an hour to go, the Lions were 17–9 clear, having scored four tries to three penalty goals. New Zealand had never threatened their guests' line and seemed content to wait for the penalties to come Clarke's way.

The usually partisan New Zealand crowd were venting their displeasure at the manner in which the All Blacks were approaching the Test. Even their forwards, who admittedly were handicapped by injuries to two of their back row, found the Lions pack a handful.

A penalty for a dubious offence offered Clarke the chance to reduce the deficit and with a siege gun kick the big full back sent the ball straight as a die between the uprights from 50 yards. A few minutes later and from a similar distance he brought the score back to 17–15 with a penalty after a lineout offence. Even the New Zealand crowd were cheering the Lions on now, cries of 'Red, Red, Red' regularly rising from the spectators packed into the tight Carisbrook enclosures.

Referee Allan Fleury, in his only international appointment, caught Gordon Wood (father of current Ireland hooker, Keith) offside at a ruck 30 yards from the posts five minutes from time. Clarke stepped forward to land another goal and thus clinched the match for New Zealand. At 18–17, the All Blacks had scored six penalties to four tries.

As the Lions attacked desperately for the winning score in the closing minutes, the onlookers got even more firmly behind them. The doyen of New Zealand press critics, Terry McLean, observed: 'The crowd in its shame called again for the Lions to win.' A last minute Lions attack carried play to the New Zealand line where a shrill blast on the referee's whistle led those supporting the tourists to think that a richly deserved fifth try had been awarded. But no. Instead, the referee had spotted

161

another Lions offence, ruling that Roddy Evans had handled in a loose scrum, and with virtually the last act of the afternoon Clarke booted the ball into touch.

Then began the inquests. More than 20 penalties had been awarded during the course of the match: 14 to the All Blacks and seven to the Lions. 'We wuz robbed,' said the British critics following the tour. Welsh journalist Bryn Thomas, barely concealing his disappointment in a byline for a New Zealand newspaper, wrote, 'Today's match will certainly live on as one of the most exciting and, indeed, unusual of all time.'

Even parts of the New Zealand media sympathised. Referring to the penalties that resulted from technical offences, Fred Boshier in the *Evening Post* concluded, 'It is tossing too much into the lap of fortune when a purely involuntary action giving no advantage to a team carries a three-point penalty while a deliberately obstructive act pays the same price or even escapes scot-free.' Thus started the campaign that 17 years later led to the introduction of the differential (free kick) penalty.

As far afield as South Africa there was sympathy for the Lions. 'Lions lose – a crying injustice,' was the headline in one daily while Okey Geffin, who in 1949 had kicked five penalties for the Springboks in a winning Test against the All Blacks, spoke for thousands of like-minded neutral rugby followers when he said, ' A side which scores four tries and does not have its line crossed does not deserve to lose.'

The debate about the merits of changing the scoring values for penalty goals and tries was well and truly launched that day though it took another dozen years for the International Board to finally increase the value of the try to four points. Under that revised scoring system, the Lions would have taken this first Test 21–18 – which would have been a much fairer reflection of the run of play.

THE LONG ARM OF THE LAW TRIES TO INTERVENE

WANGANUI, AUGUST 1959

One of the hardest earned victories by the Lions in New Zealand in 1959 was against Wanganui. Bev Risman gave the tourists the lead with a penalty goal in the fifth minute but the determined hosts equalised when their wing, Boswell, landed a similar score. A tough, uncompromising forward battle developed in which no quarter was asked and certainly none was given.

Shortly before half-time Risman was given the opportunity to regain the lead for the Lions with a penalty awarded on the Wanganui 10-yards-line. As the English fly-half began making his preparations there was a commotion among the crowd on the far side of the pitch near the home side's 25. Unknown to the referee they were trying to draw his attention to the fact that the touch-judge's flag was up to indicate that an earlier line-out had been awarded.

As Risman steadied himself to take the kick the baying from the crowd reached a crescendo. A policeman on patrol along the kicker's side of the field moved in at this stage and tapped the referee on the shoulder to point out the cause of the disturbance. The referee had lost sight of his touch-judge in the far distance against the jumbled background of faces.

What followed was more extraordinary. The official permitted Risman to take his penalty and a low-trajectory kick just scraped over the crossbar. As the Lions withdrew to their half to receive the kick-off, the referee moved across to the touchline and spoke with the touch judge, whereupon he disallowed the penalty and whistled for a line-out.

The Lions and their small band of press followers were dumbfounded by these events and it was to the players' credit that they picked themselves up to grind out a narrow 9–6 win in the second half.

THE AMAZING MONSIEUR DROP

PARIS, APRIL 1960

Paris in the spring was a painful experience for many rugby international teams visiting either the old Stade Colombes or Parc des Princes for end-of-season Five Nations matches against the French. One of France's earliest April successes was against Ireland in 1960, when a side that was playing for a share of the International Championship title ran riot, winning 23–6.

The French played fluent rugby but it was the remarkable feat of hotelier Pierre Albaladejo that made the match a memorable one. The Dax fly-half, who after winning his first cap against England in 1954 had been in the Test wilderness until the Welsh match a few weeks earlier, sent over three sweetly struck drop goals, two with his left foot and one with his right. Never before in the annals of international rugby had a player planted three dropped goals in one match. One newspaper marvelling at his accuracy, described him potting 'with the mathematical certainty of a Joe Davis sinking the last three colours in an important break.'

Albaladejo later became the voice of French televised rugby until taking a well-earned retirement in 1999 after commentating on the Five Nations Championship's final weekend. But back in the spring of 1960, he must have created something akin to a record. For, apart from his well-publicised three goals in the Stade Colombes international against Ireland, he had a couple of weeks earlier landed four drops, two off each foot, playing for Dax in the Du Manoir tournament. Moreover, a week after his Paris exhibition, he popped over two more playing for France against Italy in Treviso.

Nine dropped goals in three matches: not bad for a player who was reported as having flat feet and fallen arches and who allegedly wore specially-supported shoes in everyday life.

ROLE REVERSAL

From the beginning the aim of the Barbarians, the world's best-known wandering rugby club, was to embrace imaginative and open rugby on the field with a spirit of comradeship and conviviality off it. This aim has remained the Barbarian ideal ever since.

In 1948 came one of the red-letter days in the club and rugby's history. The Third Wallabies of that year wished to return home via Canada, where they planned to put on a couple of exhibition games in British Columbia. To raise funds to assist the tourists' cause, the Four Home Unions committee met in Edinburgh and came up with the brilliant idea of inviting the Barbarians to select a team to meet the Wallabies. Club and international rugby in Wales immediately after the war had proved a compelling draw for returning servicemen, so the choice of venue for what was regarded as an experimental match was naturally Cardiff.

The game, played before 40,000 spectators, was a rip-roaring success and an exciting spectacle played according to the Barbarians' custom. It also set an important precedent: subsequent major visiting sides have always scheduled engagements with the club as their final tour match. The fixtures became cherished features of the Barbarian tradition and invariably turned out to be memorable exhibitions of attacking rugby – a shining example of the Barbarian ideal.

With one notable exception.

The 1960–1 Fifth Springboks tour to Britain and Ireland

approached their Barbarian match at the end of a long, unbeaten tour in which there had been criticisms levelled that an invincible record was more important to them than the manner in which they played the game. Playing power rugby together with the time-honoured South African principle of subdue and penetrate, the visitors had won few friends on tour despite compiling an enviable record.

During the winter of 1960–1 an influenza epidemic swept through Britain, striking down all in its path. The tourists were no exceptions and in the week before the final match of the British leg of their tour, injuries together with illness had decimated their squad.

Consequently, Ferdie Bergh, the Springboks' tour manager, suggested to the Barbarians that, instead of the normal challenge, the fit South Africans should integrate with a Barbarian selection and play a gala match on the Arms Park. Brigadier Glyn Hughes politely yet firmly replied for the Barbarians. 'The real attraction of this game is fifteen South Africans against fifteen Barbarians. In any case, as we have always stressed [in the Barbarians], the result is of minor importance,' he said.

Despite their difficulties with injuries and illness, the South Africans were still able to field a fifteen that included no fewer than a dozen Test players. Ironically, it was the Barbarians who suffered more through late withdrawals. The Welsh full-back Terry Davies dropped out with influenza, Cyril Davies withdrew through injury on the eve of the match, and a couple of hours before kick-off the Irish scrum-half, Andy Mulligan, also went down with 'flu.

But such was the Barbarians' determination to win this match that they threw tradition to the wind. Under the captaincy of Ronnie Dawson, who had led the Lions in Australia and New Zealand two years earlier, they proceeded instead to play as if this were a fifth Test. Their tackling and defence work were watertight and it was significant that from an early stage in the match their halves, Richard Sharp and Billy Watkins, kicked as frequently as they would have done in a normal international. Gone was the ideal of attractive open rugby.

By contrast, and to their eternal credit, the Springboks ignored this defensive play and adopted the tactics more often associated with the Baa-Baas. They engaged in a wide passing game that won them many friends in a capacity 60,000 crowd. Ken Jones in the *Sunday Express* hit the nail on the head when he reported: 'We expected the dour Springbok approach to Test rugby and from the Barbarians the classical open football for which they are famous. But strange as it may seem the reverse happened. The Springboks opened up the game at every opportunity.'

Yet, despite living off emergency rations of possession, the Barbarians won a famous victory. Tries by Derek Morgan and Haydn Morgan in the eleventh and twenty-eighth minutes respectively took the club into a 6–0 lead that was held until half time.

Surprised that the Barbarians had shown so little in the way of adventurous running, the South African skipper Avril Malan continued to take the game to the club side in the second half, but to no avail. Twice Haydn Mainwaring, the uncapped Swansea replacement for Terry Davies, carried off try-saving tackles that went into the game's lore as two of the best of all time.

The first of these came when Malan, 15 stone of prime South African beef, went galloping 30 yards down the south touchline from a lineout. Only the full-back stood between the Springbok captain and a certain try. Mainwaring lined his target up and bowled him into touch with a fair and perfectly timed shoulder charge that completely knocked the stuffing out of the big South African. Poor Malan lay prone in the Cardiff mud on the sidelines for the best part of two minutes before bravely continuing. Later, Mainwaring again saved the day for the Barbarians by bringing down Michel Antelme in open field. Consequently, the score remained at 6–0.

And so the Springboks lost their unbeaten record to the good men of Barbaria but, as Vivian Jenkins summed up for the *Sunday Times*, 'They [South Africa] might well quibble that the Barbarians' alleged open football was something of a myth.'

THE GALE FORCE MATCH

WELLINGTON, AUGUST 1961

Wellington's reputation as the windy city was confirmed during the first French tour of New Zealand in 1961. The second Test of the series was staged at the city's Athletic Park stadium. It was to be the scene for the worst conditions ever witnessed in nearly 130 years of international rugby.

That same weekend, the *Canberra*, on her maiden voyage, was unable to dock at Wellington harbour due to the high winds. The film tape of the match survives and clearly shows the effects of a southerly gale that whipped up on the eve of the Test. At times the posts were crazily swaying as wind speeds reached 80 mph, the touch flags were blown over almost parallel to the pitch and kicks into the wind curled like boomerangs. The recently erected double-decker Millard stand, a sky-scraper that was designed to seat 12,000, was deemed too dangerous for spectators to sit at its southern end, though as it was, only a quarter of those who had bought tickets for the game attended.

France played with the hurricane in the first half but were unable to force a score. Everyone expected the All Blacks to prevail in the second half with the wind in their favour and still playing tricks. On one occasion the French fly-half, Pierre Albaladejo, one of the game's most accomplished kickers, kicked from his own 25 only to see the ball blown back to his own in-goal area. He even resorted to place-kicking penalties to touch, using a colleague to steady the ball.

The opening score came only 15 minutes from the end when

170

France launched an attack from their own half. Jean Piqué ran left before passing to Jean Dupuy around half-way. The little left-wing ran strongly into the gale and won the race to score in the corner. A couple of minutes later Kel Tremain equalised when he charged down a French attempt to clear and flopped on the loose ball for a try. Don Clarke, with a magnificent effort from a wide angle, converted and New Zealand were able to scrape home for a 5–3 win.

Wilson Whineray, the experienced New Zealand captain said, 'The conditions were the worst I have played under.' And those with longer memories unanimously agreed with him. 'Terrible,' said old-timer Billy Wallace, whose All Black career stretched back to 1903.

The only other comparable big match affected by gales was in Britain and also involved the All Blacks, this time at Stradey Park in October 1989. The Llanelli officials had erected a temporary stand opposite the main grandstand for the match, but the conditions were considered too dangerous for its use. Instead, the extra spectators were packed on to the terraces where they had to endure gale force winds and driving rain. After the match, spectators making their way back into the town centre found several roads closed by the police for safety reasons as slates and masonry fell off buildings and crashed to the ground. Further along the coast, the Severn Bridge was closed for twelve hours. New Zealand won that game too: 11–0.

Had these matches not involved tour sides on tight schedules, both would have been cancelled.

MOTHER'S DAY

TIMARU, AUGUST 1961

Rugby can be an aggressive game at the best of times. With thirty young players all striving to establish themselves in the hurly-burly of a contact sport played at speed, is it any wonder that tempers are occasionally frayed? But when spectators get angry and become physically involved in the action on the field then the line has to be drawn.

During France's tour of New Zealand in 1961, the French team were embroiled in brawls in several games. Strong refereeing was often required to cool eager forwards as the temperature began to rise. One game in particular, against South Canterbury at Timaru, stood out for the rough play involved.

South Canterbury had never beaten a touring side but in front of 23,000 this was to be their day. Their mobile forwards completely disrupted the French, whose tour form hit rock bottom in this match and the home side, who ran out 17–14 winners despite finishing with only 14 men, led from an early stage.

Trouble broke out at the line-outs during the second half. Barging and pushing escalated into fisticuffs and it was the French who bore the brunt of referee Pat Murphy's ire. By the end of the game the penalty count went 17–4 against the tourists who were lucky not to have had a player sent off.

But the most astonishing incident occurred near the end of the match after South Canterbury's second five-eighth, Eddie Smith, was felled by a stiff arm tackle. Michel Crauste, the

French captain, incensed the crowd further by picking the listless Smith up by the scruff of his neck and promptly dropping him back to the ground – whereupon a 56-year-old woman in the crowd rushed out from her seat, spoke to Crauste and clouted him on the back of his neck with her clenched fist.

Two policemen had to intervene before escorting her, amid loud and approving cheers, from the field. Afterwards, the mother from Oamaru explained that she felt the tactics of the French team 'were totally uncalled for. I was so mad I did not know what I was doing. I hit him hard, but I don't think it hurt. I think he got a bit of a shock though.' Attending the match with her husband, two children and nephew, she added in her defence: 'It was not good for young boys to see that sort of play.'

Monsieur Crauste's reaction to the irate woman is not on record.

SEVENTY-FIVE SECONDS TO TAKE A KICK

TWICKENHAM, JANUARY 1962

A scoreless draw in an international match would be hard to imagine nowadays. The 2000 Six Nations Championship, for instance, yielded 803 points at an average of 53.5 a match – surpassing the previous Championship best in 1997 when, in the old Five Nations, 511 points were scored at 51.1 a match.

The last nil-nil results in Tests took place in the early 1960s when there were three in consecutive seasons. Scotland and New Zealand were involved in 1964, Ireland and England in 1963 and, in 1962 at Twickenham, England and Wales also failed to score a point between them.

But not without trying – and certainly not without trying the patience of the capacity crowd assembled on a frosty January Saturday.

The story of that match is briefly told. Wales had a seasoned pack and dangerous, attacking backs. England contained their visitors up front and the home back-row tied up the Welsh halves. Result, stalemate.

Before Twickenham became the concrete arena that it is today, it was a quaint yet homely stadium, with two tall stands along the East and West touch-lines and a single-decker North Stand behind a goal-line. The South, which was open, was always a massive terrace of colourful humanity on international match days. But this architectural layout was infamous for the swirling conditions it created on the pitch for place kickers.

The Twickenham swirl struck with a vengeance as far as the

Welsh were concerned in 1962. The new Wales full-back was a young Llanelli product, Kelvin Coslett. Poor Kel made five penalty attempts at Twickenham, missing the lot, although it should be added in mitigation, that some were from long range.

Unfortunately he became more nervous as the game progressed and his haul of misses increased. At the best of times he was renowned for his meticulous preparations for place kicks in club matches. But in this game, as each kick became more and more vital to Wales's cause, so he appeared to take longer and longer over teeing up his shots. The English element in the crowd took exception to this after his second miss and began slow hand-clapping his subsequent adjustments. By his fourth attempt they were ironically jeering him.

No wonder. From the moment he dug his heel in until his boot met the ball, his action was timed at fully 75 seconds. Mercifully his fifth failure required ten seconds less to prepare.

Subsequently, the International Board laid down limits for the time spent by kickers setting up goal attempts.

EIGHT TRIES FOR HEEPS

QUIRINDI, MAY 1962

To score eight tries in a match for your country is a phenomenal feat. It requires good hands, an eye for the opening and a good turn of speed. These were qualities which New Zealand's left wing, Rod Heeps, had in abundance when the All Blacks took on Northern New South Wales early in their tour to Australia in 1962. The visitors went on to register the first ton of points by a nation on a major tour, and Heeps himself set the world record for most tries in such a match.

The welter of scoring began in the first minute when burly full-back, Don Clarke, landed a penalty goal. The Waikato wonder kicker finished the match with 23 points on a day when all but two of the New Zealand team were on the score-sheet.

Heeps, a 24–year-old pharmacist who played his provincial rugby with Wellington, was the New Zealand 100 yards sprint champion at the time. Sprinters do not always make ideal rugby wingers, but Heeps showed that he had cultivated all the skills that go to make a first-class rugby threequarter. Apart from pace, he had a good eye for the gap, a strong swerve and made tackles of textbook rectitude in defence.

He scored the first try of the match at Quirindi in the eighth minute and, with scores coming thick and fast, he went over again four more times before the interval, by which time the score was 45–0. When the last of his three second-half tries was converted the New Zealanders reached 100 points. Don McKay finished the scoring with a try to make the final score

103–0: 22 tries (valued at three points each at this time), 17 conversions and a penalty goal.

Heeps's record stands to this day for a tour match by a major International Board (IB) country visiting another IB country. However, the player faded from the scene almost as quickly as he had arrived. The meteor of 1962, he played all five Tests for New Zealand against Australia that year but, despite appearing in the trials for the following season, he never again represented his country.

THE HANGOVER MATCH

DUBLIN, NOVEMBER 1962

The dark winter days of February and early March 1962 were gloomier than usual for the folk of South Wales. A smallpox outbreak in the area threatened to disrupt community life and doctors' surgeries were besieged by thousands wishing to be vaccinated against the disease.

Sport, and rugby union in particular, was disrupted by the epidemic. Wales were due to travel to Lansdowne Road on 10 March for a Five Nations fixture with Ireland, but out of consideration for their hosts the Welsh Rugby Union agreed to a postponement, even though many Welsh rugby enthusiasts made the weekend visit to Dublin as they were unable to rearrange bookings.

Later, in Cardiff, the Medical Officer of Health gave the go-ahead for the French to fulfil their fixture with Wales at the Arms Park on 24 March and this went ahead. In due course, the Welsh Rugby Union and Irish authorities agreed to rearrange their match for 28 April on the last weekend of the season, the only practicable date available.

Early in April, however, there was a fresh outbreak of smallpox in the Bridgend area. Swansea's Football League match against Liverpool was called off and other sports were hit by renewed fears of the disease spreading. At length, the Welsh Rugby Union were again contacted by their Irish counterparts requesting a further postponement to the beginning of the following season.

Finally, on 17 November, eight months later than

scheduled, the sides met on a cold autumn afternoon in Dublin to play out the hangover match from the previous season's campaign. Wales recalled Bryn Meredith from retirement to lead them to a 3–3 draw and Ireland were left holding the Wooden Spoon. But never before nor since has the International Championship finished in the season after it started.

THE PRODUCTIVE MISS

PARIS, JANUARY 1963

The history of international rugby is littered with tales of heroic last-minute winning dropped goals. Between the wars Scotland's Herbert Waddell made a habit of pipping opponents on the wire with an accurately struck goal. More recently Michael Kiernan of Ireland and Rob Andrew of England landed dropped goals that mattered in big internationals.

Conversely, there have been matches where a late drop at goal stood out because it missed. In the Arctic winter of 1963, France and Scotland met in a temperature of ten below zero to launch the Five Nations Championship at the Stade Colombes ground north-west of Paris. Scotland played above their game and, with the wind in the second half, were holding France at 6–6 as the game drew to its conclusion.

Then, Ken Scotland, captaining his country for the first time, fielded a loose ball deep inside his own half and put in a magnificent left-footed punt to flight the ball fully fifty yards to touch on the French 25. Could the Scottish team launch one last attack and become the first side to beat France in Paris since 1958?

Their fly-half Iain Laughland evidently thought so. A maul formed from the line-out and the Scottish pack managed to recycle the ball to their scrum-half who in turn passed to Laughland. His captain had opened Scotland's account with an almost impossible drop goal from near touch on half-way only 20 minutes earlier. Now, as Laughland steadied himself, it was evident that he felt he could round off the day from a shorter range with a similar attempt.

But he completely topped his kick. A most inept drop-goal attempt sent the ball at barely shoulder height across the field towards the left corner flag, where the French right-wing Pierre Besson was waiting to field it. The wicked bounce of the rugby ball, however, tricked the Frenchman and there, flashing up at top speed was Scotland's own right wing, Ronnie Thomson, to gather the ball and dive through Besson's tackle for the winning points.

Thomson explained later that he had anticipated Laughland slanting a diagonal punt for that corner, which is why he had deserted his normal post and crossed wings. At the same time he admitted that his score – Scotland's first try in Paris for a decade – was a glorious fluke.

'What? Best drop kick I've ever made,' grinned the cheerful Laughland when told of Thomson's comment.

ARCTIC MATCH

CARDIFF, JANUARY 1963

It was the match that went down in the annals of the game as England's last win in Cardiff for 28 years. Yet at the time it was that great old English conversation point, the weather, that dominated the headlines before and after the match.

As Britain shivered through its coldest winter for 16 years, the sports-starved public wondered anxiously whether the Cardiff match would go ahead. For five weeks the football league programme and club rugby schedule had been virtually obliterated by snow and frozen grounds. The poor San Isidro Rugby Club from Argentina, who were undertaking a short tour of southern England, had spent their first Saturday shopping for duffel coats in Oxford Street, as they tried to keep the Arctic winter out of their bones, and the hardest battle they encountered throughout their tour was keeping warm.

The Cardiff groundsman, Albert Francis, helped by staff from nearby Ninian Park and volunteers from the South Wales branch of the National Association of Groundsmen, ensured that the match would go ahead. They removed an overcoat of 30 tons of straw from the pitch on the morning of the match, leaving a thin layer to protect the turf against the biting wind until an hour or so before kick off. Workmen toiled hard to salt the terraces and clear snow so that the capacity crowd could be safely accommodated. The dead ball lines, however, were shortened to only six yards from the goal lines because of frozen patches near the east and west terraces. Indeed, during the pitch preparations the paint used for marking out the lines had frozen.

182

The players' preparations for the match did not go smoothly. The Welsh side were unable to find any surface in Cardiff on which it was safe to hold a training session, though down at Porthcawl the England squad donned pullovers, scarves and tracksuits for a runabout on the sands. England reaped the benefit of that workout the next day, their fifteen appearing better able to cope with the conditions than the rustier Welsh.

On the afternoon of the match itself, the National anthems were played in the absence of the teams so that the players did not have to stand around in the cold, but could start the game immediately they marched out. The sides were issued with thermal underwear and the Welsh backs were offered mittens.

The match attracted a huge television audience and turned out to be a fascinating affair. The temperature was measured at minus six at kick off and the pitch began to freeze early on, causing players to slip and slide but adding to the excitement for spectators. Wales had several chances to score tries in the first ten minutes but handling errors robbed them of points. England went ahead just before half time with a try scored by Peter Jackson from a long Jim Roberts throw in and fully deserved their final 13–6 winning margin.

Afterwards the debate raged as to whether the match should have been played. Fortunately nobody was seriously injured, though several finished with cuts, grazes and friction burns. Only once since, when France and Ireland met in Paris in 1978, have ground conditions approached the concrete-hard danger of that Cardiff afternoon nearly forty years ago. In Paris, it was the French Federation who overruled the concerns of players, Irish officials and the referee and insisted on staging the game. 'It was a miracle no one was seriously hurt,' said the Welsh referee on that occasion.

ONE HUNDRED AND ELEVEN LINEOUTS

MURRAYFIELD, FEBRUARY 1963

The one ground in Britain where every rugby match was guaranteed to proceed during the Big Freeze of 1963 was Murrayfield. The Scottish Rugby Union in its wisdom had installed underground electric heating there a couple of years earlier ensuring that the playing surface for big matches was always excellent, no matter what weather conditions prevailed overhead.

Wales desperately wanted to win against Scotland in February 1963, having been beaten by England at Cardiff a month earlier while fielding an experimental fifteen that included six new caps. In particular, captain Clive Rowlands, who was one of those new caps, was determined to avoid leading Wales to two successive defeats.

As a leader he had a single-minded attitude to winning. Praise or scorn were irrelevant to him if his side was successful. He also wanted to dispel once and for all the theory that Murrayfield was a Welsh bogey ground. Four times since 1953, strong Welsh fifteens had journeyed to Edinburgh expecting victory only to return narrowly defeated.

For bedtime reading on the eve of the match the Welsh captain chose to study the match programme for the game. Totting up the masses of the two packs he discovered that their published statistics measured up roughly even (121 st 2 lb against Wales's 121 st 9 lb). Getting out of bed, he roused his forwards to check their weights and discovered that the two Abertillery back-row men, Alun Pask and Haydn Morgan, had had their figures considerably understated. Wales, Rowlands reckoned, would take the field with a pack that was in the region of two stones heavier than the Scots.

There and then he formulated his match plan: Wales would keep the ball among their forwards whose superior physical presence would almost certainly deliver the much-sought victory.

Rowlands, an extrovert personality whose energetic captaincy was always full of colourful gesticulations, totally ignored his backs in a match that yielded 111 line-outs – the record number for any international match. Time and again Rowlands hooked the ball into touch to push his side into Scottish territory. A Welsh supporter among their 10,000 travelling fans on Murrayfield's lofty banks was overheard saying, 'Rowlands has six signals for his backs: every one means he's going to hoof the ball back to touch.'

Wales took root in the Scottish 25 for most of the afternoon and won 6–0, Rowlands himself dropping a goal from a difficult angle in the second half. But the unattractive nature of the victory did prompt an outcry afterwards.

THE CLOSEST THING TO AN OWN GOAL

CARDIFF, FEBRUARY 1964

There is no such thing as an own-goal in rugby of course, but arguably the nearest to it in a major representative match was a remarkable score made in the tour finale played by the 1964 All Blacks against the Barbarians.

For this match the Barbarians bestowed on New Zealand's Ian Clarke honorary membership of their famous wandering club. A prop forward, Clarke had toured Britain with the 1953–54 All Blacks and had been a regular fixture in New Zealand Test packs for almost a decade when he was selected to make his second tour of Britain in 1963.

One of the front-row's typical unsung heroes, Clarke's worth to the All Blacks' XVs of his day was the unseen work that he performed in scrums, rucks and mauls. He rarely made the headlines, preferring instead to derive his pleasure from the knowledge that he had been part of a New Zealand pack that had laid the foundations for another Test victory.

By contrast his brother Don was often a match-winner with his goal-kicking feats and regularly grabbed the attention when the All Blacks were in action. For that reason, Ian's performance in the colours of the Barbarians was worthy of mention.

Clarke ran on to Cardiff Arms Park to face his countrymen wearing his own New Zealand socks, thus upholding a long-held tradition in the Barbarian club whereby players appear in their club socks. For the opening 20 minutes, matters were even with Clarke beavering away with all his usual industry even though he was facing his own tour colleagues.

Then, after a period of Barbarian pressure, the All Blacks were happy to touch the ball down for a 25-yard drop-out. Big Don Clarke took the kick sending the ball direct to Ian who was standing mid-way between the 25 and half-way. Whether or not the big Waikato brothers had planned such a move nobody bothered to enquire. Ian claimed a mark.

Now, in the days before the introduction of the free-kick clause into the game's laws in 1977, a mark or fair catch could be claimed anywhere on the field of play. Moreover, the player making the catch could elect to land a goal from a mark which was valued at three points.

To the astonishment of his team-mates (on both sides !) Ian indicated that he was going to kick for goal. Even more astonishing was the fact that the prop, who had never before drop-kicked any type of goal in a first-class match, timed his effort to perfection and sent the ball towering over the goal posts at the Taff end of the ground. His 'own goal' put the Barbarians in front and, for once, his kicking overshadowed the feats of his younger brother.

The Barbarian lead was short-lived though, as New Zealand moved ahead 6–3 by the interval and ran away to a 36–3 win by the end of the match. But Clarke's 'own goal' was the last goal from a mark seen in a major representative match on British soil.

TEN AGAINST THE HEAD

SALISBURY, JULY 1964

Ask the average hooker the result of a match after 80 minutes of hard labour at the scrum face and he will almost certainly give you a pair of figures which bear no resemblance whatsoever to the final score-line. Because for hookers, the only figures that matter in a game relate to the tight-head count: the number of heels made on the opposition's put-in.

Nowadays it is rare to see more than one or two scrums taken against the head. Even in the days of the 1950s and 1960s, when scrummaging was less of the truly specialist art that it has become today, the count rarely reached half-a-dozen. Therefore, on the occasion when it reached double figures, the feat stood out as a memorable event.

This most extraordinary hooking of modern times at representative level took place in Salisbury in July 1964 when France opened their second tour of South Africa with a fixture against Rhodesia at the capital's Police Grounds.

The opposing rakes were Ronnie Hill, already a veteran of seven Springbok Tests, and Jean-Michel Cabanier whose two French caps had come earlier the same season. The Rhodesian front-row was regarded as the most powerful in South Africa and apart from the experienced Hill, both props, Andy Macdonald and Willie van der Merwe, were Springbok trialists.

During the match, Hill took a staggering ten strikes against the head off the French. Amazingly though, the French ran out clear winners by 34–11 thanks to a superb display of goal kicking by Pierre Albaladejo.

But despite his astonishing hooking efforts, Hill could not convince the South African selectors to reinstate him and he never managed to force his way back into the Springbok Test side. For the Test against France later the same month, the selectors turned to a young new hooker from Natal named Don Walton.

As for Cabanier, he went on to win 26 caps for France before hanging up his hooking boots in 1968. But not surprisingly, perhaps, he was unable to win a place in the Test pack that beat the Springboks 8–6 in the only international of the 1964 tour.

HANCOCK'S HALF MINUTE

TWICKENHAM, MARCH 1965

Who scored Twickenham's most famous international tries? Old timers still claim that the two scored by the Russian Prince Alex Obolensky against the 1936 All Blacks on England's way to a 13–0 win would take some beating. Peter Jackson's sensational last-minute try to seize victory against the Fourth Wallabies in 1958 is still talked of today, and then there was Richard Sharp's Championship winner when he sold three outrageous dummies in the 1963 Calcutta Cup encounter. Those with shorter memories might plump for the breathtaking French try started by Pierre Berbizier and Serge Blanco on their own dead-ball-line, and finished by Philippe Saint-André under the England goal in the 1991 Grand Slam showdown.

Yet arguably the most memorable out of the blue solo effort was the 95-yard run by left wing, Andy Hancock, for England against Scotland in 1965. Scotland were leading 3–0 through a David Chisholm dropped goal and heading for their first Twickenham win since 1938 as play entered the final minute. None of the press photographers at the match rated England's chances of pulling the match out of the fire. All of them were camped in England's 25, expecting another Scotland score to seal the game.

Scotland's right wing, David Whyte, launched an attack and cutting in found himself engulfed by English forwards about 15 yards in front of England's posts. A maul developed enveloping Whyte and the ball was fed back on the England side to Mike Weston, their fly-half whose main function during the

190

afternoon had been to hoof the ball into touch. Moving left to the blind-side, he threw a pass to Hancock who was standing in isolation near the left touch line.

It was only the third pass of the match that the Northampton wing had received: he'd dropped the other two. This time he latched on to the pass and began running up the left wing. He swerved outside the Scottish back row, evaded an ineffective tackle by the Scotland full-back and raced 90 yards, hotly pursued by Iain Laughland, before lunging desperately over the line at the north end of the ground, just as the despairing Laughland completed his tackle. It was the longest solo run for a try ever seen in an international and saved England's bacon.

'I remember being helped up off the ground,' Hancock later recalled, 'but little else. On the way to the dressing room one of the spectators offered me a dram, which I gratefully accepted.'

Unfortunately, with the cameramen stranded in Hancock's wake, no press photographs of one of rugby's most famous scores exist. The only record of the try is the grainy BBC film of the move.

REFEREEING HISTORY

PARIS, MARCH 1965

Frenchmen have figured prominently in the refereeing sphere of the game in recent times. Joel Dumé and Didier Mené have been regular appointments at International Championship matches in the past decade and, before them, Georges Domercq and Francis Palmade brought a Gallic touch to the Five Nations' tournaments of the 1970s and 1980s. Respect for fair play and imaginative use of the advantage law have been the common factors running through these well-known referees' approach to important matches.

Yet before 1966 no French referee had been invited to control an international game in the Home Unions tournament. It is true that Cyril Rutherford, the administrator who did so much for French rugby in the first half of the twentieth century, did appear as a touch-judge in many of France's early internationals and actually controlled the France-England game in Paris in 1908, but he was actually Scottish born. And later, there was Jacques Muntz who was invited to referee the Four Nations match featuring England and Wales against Scotland and Ireland in 1929, when the Rowland Hill memorial gates were officially unveiled at Twickenham, but he never officiated in a Five Nations game.

In fact, it was only a fluke incident which led to French officials joining the rota for Championship games. During the 1965 France-Wales match at Stade Colombes in Paris, Ron Gilliland of Ireland had to relinquish the whistle just before half-time when he burst a blood vessel in his left calf muscle.

Pure farce followed.

Welsh and French officials joined the captains on the field to decide what course of action to take. There was no precedent nor contingent provision: this was an unknown predicament for international rugby officials. As the protagonists engaged in a prolonged and energetic debate, the presidents of the French and Welsh Unions became involved in the pandemonium, as well as the chairman of the Welsh selectors, Alun Thomas. Meanwhile, an excited party of press photographers and television camera crews strayed on to the pitch to record developments.

Touch judges at international matches up to the mid-1980s were nominated by the two participating nations. Ron Lewis for Wales and Bernard Marie of France were on duty on this occasion and were duly brought into the discussions on the field. Both were highly respected referees, but either could be considered to be biased if they took charge of the match.

The Welsh skipper, Clive Rowlands, was particularly concerned that the choice of referee should be seen as fair and unbiased as Wales, already winners of the Triple Crown, were a staggering 13–0 behind in their quest for the Grand Slam. He felt that the direct choice of a Welsh referee might infuriate the French crowd and thus pressed the point that, for fairness, the captains should spin a coin.

At length, Alun Thomas provided the voice of reason. France, as hosts he argued, had nominated the match referee, therefore they should choose the replacement. Amidst catcalls and whistles, the French touch judge was nominated and, after a ten minute interruption, play eventually resumed.

And so Monsieur Marie, a chief of the legal department with the Bank of France, took over to become the first Frenchman to officiate in the Five Nations Championship. His calm authority and scrupulous impartiality during the remainder of the match impressed everyone. 'The French referee did well,' acknowledged Clive Rowlands after his side had been beaten 22–13.

So well, in fact, that Monsieur Marie was rewarded with a

full match in the Championship the following season when England met Ireland at Twickenham. Ever since, Frenchmen have been in demand at Test level, but one wonders how long it would have taken the authorities to extend this overdue invitation had Mr Gilliland not broken down in Paris on that March afternoon 35 years ago.

TRIAL BY TELEVISION

TOULOUSE, MAY 1966

The pinnacle of the French club rugby season is the Championship final held every spring. The clubs are divided into pools that run on a league basis for two-thirds of the season, before the final stages are organised as a knock-out Cup. The rivalry is always intense and occasionally brutal.

The most infamous final was arguably that of 1966 between Agen and Dax. The opposing sides were captained by two of France's most respected players, Pierre Albaladejo and Pierre Lacroix, who as half-backs had played together 20 times for their country. Agen, having won the title the previous year, started as slight favourites with the bookmakers. Neutrals, however, wanted to see the young Dax side, who had lost three finals in a decade, take the Championship for the first time.

There was little to choose between the clubs in the early exchanges as the opening 35 minutes passed without incident. Jean-Louis Dehez put Agen in front with a penalty after 18 minutes and Albaladejo equalised with a similar score ten minutes later. The crowd were anticipating an exciting second half when, just before the interval, a huge punch-up erupted.

The match was broadcast live on French television and the cameramen zoomed in on the fracas. Away from the ball and behind the referee's back the tight forwards were engaged in a free-for-all. Arms, legs and fists were flying. No-one knew how the fights had started, but the electric atmosphere surrounding the final and the closeness of the match itself had taken effect on the packs who were clearly determined to settle old scores in a desperate attempt to establish physical superiority.

The premature whistle for half-time broke up the fracas . . . but only briefly. In the first minute of the second half the front-rows were at it again and throughout the rest of the half thuggery simmered just beneath the surface of what had turned into a very ugly spectacle. Two players were knocked unconscious, another was injured by a kick and Albaladejo was so badly shaken up that he was unable to take the conversion of Dax's late try. The match ended 9–8 in Agen's favour, but for once the money-spinning re-play of the final which normally took place as a 'friendly' on the losing team's ground (a common practice in the French Championship at the time) was banned by the French Rugby Federation (FFR).

The only re-plays were those of the television footage shown at the inquest concerning the over-vigorous play. Television for once was praised by the rugby authorities for showing the incidents in full and not ducking the issue. The French Minister for Sport was so shocked by the dirty play that the FFR was officially asked to conduct an investigation. The aftermath was that three front-row players, two from Dax and one from Agen, were banned for life. Everyone rejoiced. Trial by television had 'thrown maximum light on the cancer of brutal play'.

Interestingly, less than a year later, the three recalcitrant players had their bans lifted.

THE BATTLE OF WALDRON'S EAR

OXFORD, OCTOBER 1966

Ear-biting has brought damaging publicity to rugby at frequent intervals during the second half of the twentieth century.

Soon after the last war a brutal France-Wales clash in Paris was swept under the carpet at a time when investigative journalism had not spread to the sport. Legend has it that the Welsh prop who was the victim on that occasion formed a good friendship with the biter, and the players annually exchanged cards that read: 'Merry Christmas and a Happy New Ear.'

More recently, of course, the infamous Tetley's Bitter Cup tie between Bath and London Scottish in which the Exiles' flanker, Simon Fenn, was bitten on his left ear resulted in a protracted period of wrangling that did nothing for the reputation of the game. By then, of course, the game had turned professional and rugby union was forced to take action. It did, finding Bath prop Kevin Yates guilty and banning him for six months.

Even by 1965, when a Welsh forward allegedly bit an England player during a maul at Cardiff Arms Park, the authorities' attitudes had hardened considerably – to the extent that the Welsh Rugby Union took the then unprecedented step of dropping the alleged biter for the remainder of a Triple Crown campaign.

But, for immediate and drastic action taken after such an incident, the battle of Waldron's Ear that took place at Oxford in October 1966 marked a watershed in the game's approach to dealing with foul play.

Ollie Waldron was an Ireland forward studying nuclear physics at Merton College when he was selected to prop for Oxford University against the 1966 Wallabies. It was only the third match of the visitors' tour and they had already lost once when they turned out at Iffley Road for a mid-week match.

The students, inspired by their South African captain Tom Bedford, began confidently and opened a nine-point lead in the first twelve minutes. Australia had to wait until the second half before scoring. Jim Lenehan, their captain for the day, made a well-timed entry into the threequarter line and the upshot was a try for scrum-half John Hipwell which Lenehan, from a wide angle, converted. The Aussie captain made another incursion five minutes later to send Stewart Boyce over in the corner, and then put his side ahead after 15 minutes with a sweetly-struck dropped goal from half-way.

Thereafter, at 11–9, the match was as tight as the score suggests. Five minutes from the end came the incident that sent this game into the history books. From a scrum, Ollie Waldron emerged with a torn ear. He promptly left the field and was taken to hospital where he lost count of the number of stitches inserted in his ear-lobe.

It later emerged that Ross Cullen, the Wallaby hooker, had experienced such a torrid time in the front-row as a result of Waldron's illegal boring tactics that he had taken the law into his own hands. Waldron later stated that Cullen had threatened to bite him if he persisted in his tactics, whereupon he felt the Australian's teeth sink into his left ear-lobe.

After the match neither the referee, Peter Brook, nor Bill McLaughlin, the Wallabies' manager would comment on the incident. McLaughlin, who at the outset of the tour had promised to deal briskly with any foul play perpetrated by his team, was true to his word. The day after the match, in an unprecedented statement, he announced: 'I have decided that one of my players cannot be relied upon to carry out the firm decision of the Australian rugby touring management to play good clean rugby during the tour of the British Isles. I have therefore reluctantly decided that the player, Ross Cullen, will return at once to Australia.'

Mr McLaughlin's act was fully supported by his Union and acclaimed all-round by sports administrators and the media. 'It is easily the most significant decision ever taken in the interests of clean rugby and will have a salutary effect on the rest of the tour,' wrote the rugby correspondent of the *Daily Telegraph*.

On the evening of the announcement, as Cullen boarded the Alitalia flight for Sydney via Rome at London Airport, he vowed that he would never play rugby football again, adding, 'It's all very unfortunate but I must accept the decision.'

Back in Queensland, Cullen's home state, there was a feeling that their man was being made a scapegoat. He had never previously been involved in dirty play during a junior and senior career spanning 13 years and a week after his departure from Britain his Eastern Districts club in Brisbane unanimously re-appointed him as their captain for 1967. But Cullen stuck to his word. He never played again and disappeared from the rugby scene.

KISS OF LIFE

NEWPORT, NOVEMBER 1966

Rugby football has had its share of tragic accidents resulting in death or permanent injury of players. At the highest level of the game such incidents have been mercilessly rare, though one episode during the Newport-Australia match at Rodney Parade in 1966 could have had a more serious outcome but for the quick-thinking actions of two medics who were fortunately on hand to deal with the situation.

Newport had famously beaten Wilson Whineray's Fifth All Blacks 3–0 in 1963 and were successfully demonstrating to the Fifth Wallabies how difficult it was for visitors to win at their ground. An uneventful first 75 minutes saw Stewart Boyce score a corner try for the tourists and David Watkins a penalty goal for Newport. As the game headed for a dull draw Welsh international centre Gordon Britton was simultaneously but perfectly legally tackled by a couple of Australians. In an accidental clash of heads the Newport man collapsed in a heap to the ground.

Britton, a strapping six-foot policeman, began convulsing whilst lying on the pitch. It was then that John O'Gorman, Australia's Number Eight and a qualified doctor, rushed across and realised that the Welsh international had half swallowed his tongue and was struggling to breathe. As the Australian put his fingers into Britton's mouth to bring the player's tongue back into position, Newport's medical adviser Dr John Miles arrived quickly on the scene.

By this time Britton was in a very distressed condition. 'He was turning grey and blue and still finding it difficult to breathe,' said Dr Miles, who promptly administered mouth-to-mouth resuscitation.

The prompt action by Dr O'Gorman and Newport's adviser undoubtedly saved Britton's life. The player began breathing more easily and, though suffering severe concussion, was carried from the field on a stretcher and rushed to the Royal Gwent Hospital. Happily he was discharged no worse for wear a couple of days later.

THE UNBELIEVABLE DEBUT

CARDIFF, APRIL 1967

The Welsh rugby selectors have never flinched from throwing a good young 'un into the lion's den of Test rugby. The history of Welsh successes down the years is littered with the heroic feats of teenagers. Haydn Tanner against the All Blacks in 1935, Lewis Jones at Twickenham in 1950, Terry Davies against Scotland in 1953 and Terry Price in the Welsh Triple Crown year of 1965 were all barely out of Secondary School rugby when they confidently stamped their class on the international game.

But perhaps there was never a Five Nations debut that matched the performance of 18-year-old Keith Jarrett against England at Cardiff in 1967. The Newport player had left Monmouth School only a couple of months earlier before finding himself selected in the unaccustomed position of full-back for an international against an England side that was seeking the Triple Crown. A centre threequarter by inclination and experience, Jarrett was chosen out of position by a Welsh selection committee that was desperate to accommodate a reliable place kicker.

Young Jarrett did not let them down. He was an old-fashioned, straight-on place kicker who tended to tilt the ball forward as he teed it up. He kicked his first penalty from near the left touchline early in the match. The ball appeared to be veering away to Jarrett's right before striking a post and bouncing over the crossbar. After that, the boy could do no wrong. The goal gave England a taste of what was to come.

202

Wales led 14–6 at half time but by midway through the second half they were only four points ahead at 19–15, with England growing in confidence. Then England won a lineout in front of the south stand at the Westgate Street end of the ground and, from his own 25, Colin McFadyean, the English centre, kicked high towards his opponents' half with a kick designed to test the inexperienced Welsh full-back. Positionally, Jarrett was completely exposed. He had stood too far back to take the ball on the full and had no option but to let it bounce high on the half-way line. The English threequarters and loose forwards were steaming across the field, hoping to take advantage, when Jarrett shot into view and perfectly timed his run to take the ball on the bounce and set off full pelt along the north touchline.

On and on he pounded with scarcely a hand laid on him. Once into the 25 it was obvious that no one would catch him and with no Welsh player in support he completed his 50-yard solo effort with a try in the corner that brought the house down. To add insult to injury, Jarrett converted from the touchline, bouncing the ball over off the top of an upright.

By the end of normal time Wales were 34–15 ahead, though England managed two late scores in injury time to add a touch of respectability to the result. Jarrett kicked seven goals from eight attempts – his one failure of the afternoon hit a post – and equalled the Welsh international record for most points (19) in a match, set by Jack Bancroft against a fledgling French side 57 years earlier.

The only comparable Test debut by such a youngster was made by the New Zealand wing Jeff Wilson against Scotland at Murrayfield in 1993. Brought on tour more for the experience than as a front line Test player, Wilson found himself promoted to the Test team at barely 20 years of age and scored a hat trick of tries in a record 51–15 walloping.

FOUR DRAWS IN FIVE MATCHES

HARTLEPOOL, APRIL 1967

The first county rugby match was staged at Leeds in 1870 with Lancashire defeating Yorkshire by a goal and two tries to nil. In 1883, regulations governing playing qualifications were agreed by the English counties and in 1889 the first championship officially sanctioned by the Rugby Football Union was introduced. Yorkshire were the inaugural winners.

The first formal structure to the Championship was imposed the following year: the north-east, north-west, south-east and south-west produced four group winners who then met in a league round to produce a title winner. In 1895 the structure was modified to produce a knockout phase which led to a final tie.

The competition produced its hundredth climax in June 2000, but the most unusual run of results in its colourful history came in 1967 when Surrey were the finalists with Durham. Draws have always been rare in senior rugby but that season the Surrey side featured in four draws in their final five matches. They had also drawn earlier in the season with Middlesex in the regional league.

Their semi-final was against Cornwall. The Duchy always treats its county side with the same respect that the rest of England reserves for the national team. (Indeed, nowadays the Twickenham authorities pray for Cornwall to reach the final every year to ensure a bumper gate). Matters were no different in 1967 when Surrey journeyed west to Redruth on 4 February for their first showdown with Cornwall.

At the time Cornwall were spoilt for choice at full-back where they had at their disposal Roger Hosen and Graham Bate, two fine players with differing talents. Hosen was the England full-back at the time and a siege gun kicker who could place goals from anywhere inside his own half. Bate was more agile about the field but a less accomplished kicker. In the event, Bate was given the nod for the Redruth match.

The match went down in Cornish lore as the one that got away. The western county scored two tries but Bate's big failure with six kicks at goal – two conversions and four penalties – cost Cornwall dear. For big Bob Hiller, with a couple of penalty goals for Surrey, retrieved the draw and enabled the visitors to live to fight another day.

Hosen was recalled for the replay a fortnight later at Richmond. And it was a good job too, as far as Cornwall were concerned. Surrey took a 14–3 lead before Cornwall staged a magnificent comeback and, with the last act of the game, Hosen landed a touchline conversion to square the scores at 14-all. So it was back to Redruth for the second replay which, this time, Surrey comfortably won 14–3, to reach their first final for seven years.

Having reached the final, Surrey were involved in two further draws. The final against Durham took place at Twickenham, where Bob Hiller kicked 11 of their 14 points in a drawn game. The replay in late April was staged at Hartlepool and when this ended scoreless, the two counties were called on by the authorities to discuss the next step, there being no such thing as extra time or penalty shoot-outs to produce instant winners in those days. The sides debated the logistics of another replay but, with only a week to the end of the official season, they decided to share the title. It was, everyone agreed, the most spectacular ending to a county championship campaign.

X CERTIFICATE RUGBY

KIMBERLEY, AUGUST 1967

So rough and nasty was the Griqualand West v France tour match at Kimberley in August 1967 that the public outcry after the match had officials seriously considering imposing age restrictions, similar to the X certificate ratings system used in films, for admittance to rugby matches.

France toured South Africa that year as Five Nations champions and their mid-week match against the Griquas was billed as the biggest provincial game of the tour. More than 14,000 attended, including in the region of 5,000 school-children and three of the South African Test selection committee. The Griquas were unbeaten in the domestic Currie Cup tournament, and in Piet Visagie and Mannetjies Roux they had two of the linchpins of the Springbok Test side.

The match turned into a brawl, with the referee, Captain P A 'Toy' Myburgh, frequently having to exert his authority over the forwards in an ill-tempered game. Players swapped punches, blows and kicks and Alain Plantefol, one of the French locks, required stitches to a cut inflicted during one fracas. The big Frenchman was also warned by the referee that he faced a sending off offence, after one particular incident near the end of the match.

During one flurry of fists the referee himself was punched twice. Whether the blows were intentional or not was unclear, for he refused to comment on the incident afterwards, despite conceding that the match was the roughest he had ever handled.

206

The constant fighting roused the crowd into a frenzy and it was this fact that prompted Morrie Zimerman, one of the the Springbok selectors present at the match, to decry matters after the final whistle. 'I regret that more than 5,000 children watched this exhibition,' he told the *Cape Times* in an interview. 'The censors restrict certain films to age groups because they were not fit to be seen by children. The stage is now being reached when rugby matches such as the one witnessed today fall into this category.'

REFEREE SENT OFF

PLYMOUTH, NOVEMBER 1967

According to the Rugby Law book, the referee has the power to order off a touch judge who in his opinion is guilty of misconduct. It doesn't happen very often, but when it does occur you can bet your bottom dollar that the event will make news.

In November 1967, the Royal Naval Engineering College and Camborne were involved in a friendly club match at Plymouth. George Riches, a well respected referee in the south-west, a regular official on the county championship circuit and a former member of England's international panel, was running the line for Camborne when, early in the second half, there was a touchline incident.

A couple of forwards became entangled in a punch up and the well-meaning Riches dashed in to intervene. By the time he arrived on the scene, the two fighters were going at it hammer and tongs and he knew that in order to make his presence felt, he would have to separate them forcibly. So he put his arm around the offending College forward and tried to pull him back.

An incensed supporter misinterpreted the action. Thinking that Riches was having a go at the College player, the supporter ran on and jumped on Riches's back before joining in the fracas. At this point the match referee came over. He, too, mis-interpreted the situation having arrived late on the scene and told his touch judge that he was dismissing him for fighting. There was some confusion about the dismissal but it was confirmed later.

'The referee did send him off,' said the Camborne secretary, Arthur Kemp, after the match. 'But from what I saw of the incident this was not necessary. George was only trying to keep the peace.'

B TEST DAMPENS POST-MATCH ENTHUSIASM

CARDIFF, DECEMBER 1967

The 1967 All Blacks tour of Europe was due to finish in December with two matches in Ireland. Unfortunately, owing to an outbreak of foot and mouth disease, the tourists were prevented from leaving the mainland and had to forego their visits to Dublin and Belfast. As there were several farmers in the New Zealand party, they no doubt understood the reasons for the cancellation.

As it turned out, the change of plan proved a blessing in disguise for some fans. The last match on the mainland was scheduled for Cardiff Arms Park on 9 December, when the tourists were to have played East Wales. A heavy blanket of snow, however, covered Cardiff that weekend causing the match to be postponed. But the cancellation of the Ireland leg of their tour meant that the Cardiff match could be re-scheduled for mid-week and, as a suitable thaw set in, the game duly went ahead.

East Wales became the first side to hold the tourists, with Gareth Edwards's team forcing an honourable 3–3 draw in which the teams scored a try apiece. Opinion after the match was that the All Blacks had been lucky to escape with the draw. East Wales had fluffed five kicks at goal, there was a palpable penalty try disallowed when Fergie McCormick obstructed Keri Jones and Barry John's last-minute drop at goal was an inch wide of making history.

All were agreed that the match was the outstanding one of

the tour, full of skilful rugby and exciting to the very end. But where did everyone go afterwards?

A draw against the All Blacks in Cardiff would normally be the prompt for the good people of Wales to make a rush to drink the capital's pubs dry. But Cardiff on the night of Wednesday 13 December, 1967, was virtually deserted. The after-match atmosphere in the streets was the strangest ever witnessed in the city.

More than 40,000 had taken time off work, school or buried their grannies once again to get to see the All Blacks. Special catering arrangements had been made at the city's big hostelries, who were expecting to be inundated with supporters after the game. So what was the reason for the abstinence? Apparently, the recently introduced breathalyser test. It clearly had its desired effect, for everyone deserted the city immediately after the game in order to celebrate at pubs within walking distance of their homes.

THE DROP THAT NEVER WAS

DUBLIN, MARCH 1968

Mike Titcomb of Bristol was a referee noted for his empathy with players during a career that took in eight major international matches between 1966 and 1972. There was an occasion in Dublin in 1968, however, when even he would be the first to admit that he had no empathy with the Irish crowd.

The occasion was the Ireland-Wales match that season when he erroneously awarded a dropped goal to each side. The first of these was in the twentieth minute of the first half when Ireland, leading 3–0, went further ahead through a drop goal from 35 yards by their fly half, Mike Gibson. The ball was touched in flight by Welsh flanker John Taylor, which should have invalidated the score, but Mr Titcomb ruled that the kick was good. Naturally, the Irish crowd did not object. Wales then pulled back a penalty goal, making the scoreline 6–3 at the break, and then equalised early in the second half with international rugby's most famous dropped goal that never was.

Gareth Edwards drop-kicked high towards the Irish posts. Practically everyone in the ground saw the ball curl at least a foot outside the upright, but poor Mr Titcomb signalled the goal. Edwards, with a cheeky piece of gamesmanship, had raised his arm high as if indicating a fine goal and the referee was clearly taken in.

The Irish players, unaware that the goal had been given, assumed their positions for a 25 drop-out. They then realised to their dismay that the Welsh team had retreated to their own

212

half, expecting a restart from half-way. Eventually it dawned on the crowd that the goal had been awarded and, as a result, a near riot resulted. Bottles and cans were hurled on to the pitch as a crescendo of hoots, whistles and boos emanated from the Lansdowne Road enclosures. Play was held up for several minutes as spectators broke through the touch-line cordons to remonstrate with the referee.

When play eventually resumed the Irish, clearly roused by the injustice, raised their game to a fever pitch and the Welsh were swept aside in the tight and loose. At length, in the ninth minute of stoppage time, Ireland's wing forward Mick Doyle crashed over for the winning try. The conversion failed but that did not matter as the whistle for no-side went immediately afterwards, leaving Ireland deserved victors by 9–6.

'I thought the ball had gone over,' Mr Titcomb innocently explained after receiving a police escort from the pitch to the safety of the dressing room at the end of the match.

At least justice was finally seen to be done that day, which is more than can be said for another match involving Wales, in 1978. In the second Test of that year's tour down under, the Grand Slam champions went down 19–17 to a late dropped goal by Australia's fly half, Paul McLean, that was hotly disputed by the Welsh players, who protested that the kick had flown six inches wide of the posts. The Australian referee would have none of it and ruled that the kick was good.

A REPLACEMENT'S HAT-TRICK

SYDNEY, JUNE 1968

Replacements for injured players were occasionally made in New Zealand v Australia Test matches, long before the International Board officially sanctioned their use in 1968. Indeed, even as far back as 1907, three replacements were made in the Sydney Cricket Ground Test between the two nations.

Replacements were still permitted between them when, in the 1947 series, an interesting qualifying restriction to their use was made. Now the replacements could only come on before half-time, presumably to discourage abuse of the law. Incidentally, in the programme for the first Test at Brisbane that year, New Zealand listed ten reserves from whom to make any necessary replacements. Even today when replacements seem to come and go with great regularity, teams nominate only seven for internationals.

The use of replacements in Australian Tests ended with the election of the Australians to the International Board in 1949. It was perhaps fitting then, given their long history of using replacements, that the first Australia v New Zealand Test under the International Boards's ruling (also at the Sydney Cricket Ground, in 1968) should be remembered for the remarkable performance of New Zealand's substitute loose forward, Ian Kirkpatrick, who in the twenty-fifth minute became his country's first replacement since that 1947 series.

Kirkpatrick came on when Brian Lochore, the New Zealand captain, withdrew with a hamstring injury. Within ten minutes

214

he had scored the first try of the match. In the second half he crossed for the last two tries of the afternoon, to become the first substitute to score a hat trick in a Test.

Kirkpatrick went on to become the most prolific try scoring forward in the history of Test rugby, though at the time of writing his record appears likely to be overtaken by England's Neil Back. Even so, in the intervening years the only other replacements to finish with three tries in a Test are Byron Hayward of Wales, who performed the feat against Zimbabwe on his debut in 1998, and Tiaan Strauss for Australia against Ireland in 1999.

One of the most unusual replacement tries in an international was scored by Maesteg's Chico Hopkins for Wales against England at Twickenham in 1970. Wales were trailing 6–13 when their star player, Gareth Edwards, was forced off through injury and on came little Chico for his only Welsh cap. First he created a blind-side opening for J P R Williams to crash over and then he popped over himself for a try that was converted to put Wales ahead. But the unique point about Hopkins's score was that it was a replacement's try awarded by a replacement referee. Monsieur Robert Calmet, the French referee, had had to retire at half-time with a broken leg and England's Johnny Johnson had come on to deputise.

More recently, since the advent of blood bin substitutions, two performances warrant mention. Eddie Halvey created a piece of rugby history for himself in the 1995 Rugby World Cup when he came on as a temporary replacement for Denis McBride in Ireland's crucial pool match against Wales. While Halvey made his cameo appearance he scored a try that helped his side to a 24–23 win and qualification for the quarter finals. Even Halvey's feat, however, was surpassed a couple of years later when Australian Mitch Hardy managed two tries whilst deputising briefly as a temporary replacement for Stephen Larkham against France at the Sydney Football Stadium.

INJURED RUNNING OUT

PARIS, JANUARY 1969

Replacements were nominated for the Five Nations Championship for the first time in 1969. In the opening match of the campaign that year, France were mightily relieved to have a bench of ready-changed substitutes on hand when a stand-in for Jean-Pierre Salut, a blond flanker of Russian extraction, was needed slightly earlier than anticipated.

Salut was a sublime loose forward who had set the Five Nations alight with his dashing play in 1968 when France won their first Grand Slam. On tour with the Tricolores in New Zealand and Australia during the summer of that year he had fallen out with the management over what was referred to as 'his excessive individualism off the field' and, as a result, the French had dropped him for their three autumn internationals against the Springboks and Romania. But he was recalled for the championship opener with Scotland and his return was looked forward to with relish by the French rugby public as well as the critics.

Alas, he was to become the victim of one of international rugby's most unfortunate incidents. He twisted an ankle before leaving the dressing room and was apparently given a pain-killing injection. Then, as he was running out he was observed to go over on the ankle on the steps leading up from the tunnel to the field and fell heavily to the ground.

Later the story emerged that Salut had only gone on to the field to show his face, for the theory held in some quarters of French rugby was that he was often a bit too quick to withdraw from international sides. It was clear, however, that he would be unable to take his place in this particular side, so the French were forced to call on one of their bench replacements even before the match started.

So, up from the bench stepped prop forward Jean Iraçabal and without batting an eyelid the French selectors proceeded to completely rearrange their scrum. Iraçabal was a specialist loose-head prop, so original selection Jean-Michel Esponda was shuffled across to tight-head. Michel Lasserre was moved from tight-head to second-row replacing Benoît Dauga, Dauga slipped back to the Number Eight slot where Walter Spanghero had been originally chosen, and Spanghero went across to fill the open-side position vacated by Salut. Five pack changes between leaving the dressing room and lining up for the National Anthem must surely be a record in a Test match. As Clem Thomas noted in the *Observer*: 'Only the French would make a change of such complexity.'

Scotland, however, showed their guts and won a match in which France displayed all their talent. A late try by Jim Telfer brought them a 6–3 win that was to be their last in Paris for 26 years.

THE GAME WITH A PUNCH

CARDIFF, MARCH 1969

Many Wales and Ireland matches down the years have been remembered more for their tough and uncompromising forward exchanges than the quality of the rugby. The 1914 showdown in Belfast, for instance, was often referred to as the 'roughest ever' by old timers. It was a game that featured a running feud between several members of the Irish and Welsh packs in which punches were exchanged off the ball and out of sight of the referee. The sides enjoyed their 80-minute scrap and though the result of the match soon became forgotten, the Welsh pack of that year who were led by the Rev Alban Davies were for ever and a day referred to as 'The Terrible Eight'.

The modern equivalent to that ancient ritual was a less cavalier affair. Moving fast forward to 1969, Wales entertained Ireland at Cardiff when the visitors were seeking the Grand Slam and Triple Crown for the first time for more than 20 years. Wales, with a new, young side that had beaten Scotland, were pioneering a squad system that season. It involved a group of 28 leading players who met regularly on Sundays under the beady eye of coach Clive Rowlands, who put the boys through their paces. The system courted controversy in the Home Unions, with the Irish being particularly outspoken about the professional approach adopted by the Welsh. Accepted practice at the time was for international teams to meet no more than 48 hours before kick-off times.

The Irish were not altogether lily white themselves going into the Grand Slam match. There had been allegations that the

French and Scots had been battered into submission by the Irish forwards earlier in the season and when the sides lined up to meet Prince Charles, a guest of the Welsh Rugby Union in his year of investiture as Prince of Wales, few expected that the ensuing game would be a vicar's tea party.

The match erupted in the third minute when the Welsh captain, Brian Price, flattened Ireland's pack leader, Noel Murphy, with a right upper-cut that would have done Henry Cooper proud. The punch was thrown in front of the main grandstand and was clearly seen by millions watching the match on television. Surely the referee, Doug McMahon of Scotland, had no alternative but to issue the Welsh captain with his marching orders?

But Mr McMahon, who had been unwell during the morning with a stomach upset and very nearly cried off from refereeing the match, did not send the Welshman off. Price was a skilful lock who had a reputation for restraint. The referee sensed that he had been sorely provoked and instead issued a severe reprimand to the effect that the captain would be off if there was a repeat of his outburst.

Even Price's best friends thought he was lucky to stay on. Former distinguished Welsh referee, Gwynne Walters, was convinced afterwards that he should have been dismissed without further warning, though Price's subsequent statements went some way towards explaining if not justifying his actions. 'A player came over the top in a maul and his fingers were in my eyes. You don't hang about,' he said. Murphy denied that he had clawed Price.

The niggling persisted throughout the first half. Three Irish forwards, Murphy (again), Ken Kennedy and Jim Davidson needed further attention as the battle raged on and each finished the match suffering from concussion. Kennedy was indefensibly punched whilst pinned between his props in the front row of a scrummage. At one stage Ireland's captain, Tom Kiernan, threatened to march his side off. On the Welsh side, their big second row Brian Thomas was on the receiving end of a stray boot at the bottom of a ruck, and had to withdraw to have ten stitches inserted in a head wound, as under-cover punching and gouging continued among the packs.

The better organised Welsh XV ran away to a 24–11 victory in the second half after trailing for much of the first. Yet the roughest match ever of the television age left a bitter taste as the arguments about foul play continued long after the result had been forgotten.

BUILDING SITE RUGBY

CARDIFF, APRIL 1969

No one could accuse the Welsh Rugby Union (WRU) of sitting on its laurels as far as developing the site at Cardiff Arms Park is concerned. At regular intervals since the 1930s the Union has invested huge amounts of money into capital re-developments that have greatly benefited the rugby-loving Welsh public. The culmination, of course, is the spanking new Millennium Stadium that was unveiled for the 1999 Rugby World Cup. But the opening of the double-decker north stand (1934), the south stand upper deck extension (1956) and the ambitious re-build that turned the Arms Park into a National Stadium worthy of that title in the 1970s were equally magnificent projects in their day.

The arrangements for the re-build in the 1970s led to international rugby taking place against surely its oddest back-drop. The old north stand was pulled down over the summer of 1968 to clear the way for the first stage of the re-development – the construction of a new cantilever north stand. For the internationals of 1969, however, it meant that the ground had a reduced capacity of 29,000 on the remaining three sides of the pitch.

Wales's Triple Crown match against England in April that year took place on a ground that resembled a building site. Barbed wire fences had to be erected on the north side to keep out an expected crowd of gatecrashers and Cardiff Police joined Welsh Rugby Union officials and security experts to ensure that the perimeter fencing was not breached. The police

221

also warned that trespassers would be ejected. Meanwhile, the contractors, Andrew Scott Limited, confirmed that their work-men would be engaged in the building of the new super-structure while the match was taking place – a situation that surely would not arise today when public safety is paramount. Press photographs of the game showed, unsurprisingly, that the workforce were more distracted by the events on the field than the job in hand.

So why didn't the Welsh Rugby Union make arrangements to shift the match to Twickenham instead? In 1998 and 1999, during the construction of the Millennium Stadium, they successfully decamped to Wembley Stadium, culminating in a famous win over England, robbing Martin Johnson's men of the Grand Slam in the last ever Five Nations Championship match.

But back in 1969, Welsh rugby was riding on the crest of a wave. Cliff Jones, chairman of the Welsh selectors, explained the decision to play on the Arms Park rather than in England thus: 'We studied this problem when we were making our arrangements for this season,' he said. 'We realised that it could turn out to be a very important game in this season's championship, but we considered it would be unfair both for our team and our supporters to turn a home game into an away one.'

And so Wales delighted their fans, winning their building site Test 30–9 to carry off the Triple Crown and Five Nations Championship.

THE SECRET AFFAIR

NEW BRIGHTON, NOVEMBER 1969

The Sixth Springboks to Britain and Ireland were the last official South African international team to visit these shores for more than 20 years. Their matches were played in difficult circumstances as protesters staged anti-apartheid demonstrations inside as well as outside the venues where they were scheduled to appear.

Even before the opening match of the tour, against Oxford University, the tourists had a taste of what was to come. Anticipating demonstrators, Oxford police informed the University Rugby Club that it would be unable to guarantee safe arrangements for a match at Iffley Road. It was touch and go whether the match would proceed, but on the eve of the fixture it was announced that Twickenham would stage the game.

Two groups of protesters arrived at the ground on the afternoon of the match. There was a peaceful demonstration outside the ground but a more militant group infiltrated the spectators inside to disrupt the match by blowing whistles. The game was surrounded by confusion, though a strong police cordon successfully restricted demonstrators from breaking onto the field of play.

Similar scenes followed the tourists more or less throughout the tour. At Swansea there were unpleasant violent scenes before, during and after the Springboks' game against the local club. By the time the South Africans were due to make their first visit of the tour to Ireland in late November, concerns were being expressed that the prevailing political troubles there,

223

coupled with the threat of anti-apartheid disruption, would make the Ravenhill Ground in Belfast, where the tourists were due to play, the focus for violent groups. And so the scheduled tour match against Ulster was cancelled.

The Saturday that had been set aside for that game, however, was also the date when New Brighton, one of Northern England's most homely clubs, were due to entertain the North of Ireland Football Club, one of Ulster's oldest and most distinguished clubs. The tour committee secretly arranged for the clubs to forego their annual fixture and to field a combined fifteen that would face the Springboks instead. None of the players knew about the plans until the morning of the match. The game was played before a small crowd and went off without a hitch. It remains the only major tour match in the sport's history to be played in such secrecy.

The Springboks won 22–6 and their skipper, Dawie de Villiers, said afterwards that they had thoroughly enjoyed 'playing in a purely rugby atmosphere'. For once the tour demonstrators were absent, only learning that the game had been staged when they read the newspapers the next day.

The Springboks were to feature in an even more clandestine affair nearly a dozen years later in North America. On that occasion they were making a three-match visit to the United States after a full-scale tour of New Zealand.

In an effort to escape anti-tour groups, their international with the Eagles was hastily arranged for a secluded polo field in the country districts of New York. The pitch was littered with horse manure, the makeshift posts were rapidly erected before the match and just as quickly dismantled after it – preparations that were similar to those of a Sunday morning park match. It was recorded that 35 spectators, 20 policemen, a television crew, one pressman and no protesters attended.

KICK HIS CHAUFFEUR WHILE
YOU'RE AT IT

TWICKENHAM, FEBRUARY 1970

Tony O'Reilly began his senior rugby career on the Dublin club rugby circuit in 1954. Within months his powerful running and resourceful defence for Ireland were the talk of the Five Nations. O'Reilly was Ireland's centre, but the 1955 Lions in South Africa used him primarily as a wing. That tour made him. The red-headed teenager who used his pace to turn defences inside out finished with 16 tries to his name and played a significant part in the Lions' 23–22 win in the Johannesburg Test.

More than 95,000 were present to see him stamp his name on that game. He created a try for Scotland's Jim Greenwood and ran like an express train to score another. The Lions subsequently shared the series before returning to a heroes' welcome. In addition to his play, O'Reilly's wit also made him a popular member of the tour party. Furthermore, his good looks turned the heads of adoring South African women on that tour. An 'I-touched-Tony' following developed and there was talk later of his being approached for a part in the remake of the movie *Ben Hur*.

O'Reilly also toured with the Lions in 1959 to Australia and New Zealand. Once again, O'Reilly the rugby player was the star attraction on the field and his 22 tries on that tour remains a Lions record. And once more, he was the star off the pitch as well. By now a junior solicitor, he featured prominently in representations to management over injustices felt by the players and his witty intellect continued to amuse his colleagues.

This magnetic personality and intellectual energy took him to great success in his business career and by the age of 30 he was manager of the Irish Dairy Marketing Board and he later became president of H J Heinz. His business interests in Ireland eventually made him that country's richest man and biggest employer.

However, as far as his rugby career was concerned, the widely-held tenet was that the best of his rugby was never seen in these islands. His Ireland career was interrupted by injuries and business commitments and by 1964 his international rugby days appeared to be over. Until, that is, he was dramatically called up on the eve of the 1970 Twickenham international against England when Ireland's original wing choice, Bill Brown, withdrew from the squad with an ankle injury.

At 33, O'Reilly was enjoying his social rugby with London Irish and had clearly lost the pace and stamina of an international class threequarter. He was now considerably broader than on his Test debut 15 years earlier and after Ireland's eve-of-the-match run-out one of the squad confided that their warm-up run had involved 'running twice round O'Reilly'. The great man had actually written the lead article for the official match programme and had been invited by his old Lions colleague, Cliff Morgan, to help with the live BBC television commentary. On hearing of his sudden international recall O'Reilly announced that he was delighted to be back. His presence added another 5,000 to the Twickenham gate. It was hard luck, though, on the young travelling reserve Frank O'Driscoll of University College Dublin who, after getting so close, never won his cap for Ireland.

Unfortunately, O'Reilly spent most of the match in a daze having received a kick on the head after diving at the feet of England's pack. 'And while you're at it, why don't ya kick his chauffeur too,' remarked an Irish voice in the crowd. For O'Reilly, by then the European managing director of H J Heinz, had famously turned up for the pre-match runabout at the Honourable Artillery Club in central London in a chauffeur-driven limousine.

Despite his unremarkable play in that game, that extraordinary recall added another remarkable statistic to his file: an international career spanning 16 seasons, the world record for rugby union.

RUGBY'S LADIES FROM HELL

GOSFORTH, OCTOBER 1970

Back in September 1964 Harold Wilson was on the verge of becoming British premier and General de Gaulle was France's president when British and French followers were the first Europeans to be captivated by the sight of Fijian rugby.

Bursting with energy, the fiery and enterprising tourists passed through a ten-match tour of Wales and France like a breath of fresh air, laying to rest the then contemporary theories that rugby started and finished with defence. 'Fijians provide superb rugby spectacle,' announced *The Times* after the islanders had delighted the crowd in their 23–12 win against a combined XV at Bridgend in the opening game of the visit. The relaxed Fijians concentrated on retaining the ball and running with it, providing British crowds with the type of rugby spectacles that they had been denied for years.

The Fijians were called the 'Ladies from Hell' by the British press, on account of their bare-legged appearance in the grey-flannel skirts that were a part of their everyday wear when they arrived in Britain. There was nothing lady-like about their play, as Wales and France discovered in the two international matches that took place on the tour.

The game with Wales at Cardiff was a sell-out. The Welsh XV opened comfortably and established a sound lead before the Fijians mounted a fierce rearguard action. The final score was 28–22 to Wales, but not before a burly Fijian prop forward named Sevaro Walisoliso had brought the house down by scoring three tries.

228

On to France, then, for the second half of the tour. The Fijians played with brio to outwit a Languedoc/Pyrénées/ Roussillon Selection in Perpignan by 20–5, but were disappointed to lose 12–22 to France B before the Test at Stade Colombes on 17 October. The Test match needed a dry day and a firm pitch, but in the event showers dampened the enthusiasm of the islanders. This time it was the French who put on a late display of exuberant running rugby, scoring three tries in the last ten minutes to run out 21–3 winners, but the Fijians were by no means disgraced.

When the Fijians returned to Britain in 1970 they reserved their best performance for a match against the Barbarians staged at Gosforth. Gordon Ross described the action most poetically. 'This is what we had been waiting for!' he told the readers of the *Playfair Rugby Annual*. 'In the second half the Fijians erupted to play some brilliantly flamboyant and yet destructive rugby that brought a [29–9] victory.'

The tourists won plenty of ball and unshackled their inhibitions to play their spontaneous game. Seven tries were scored as the best British side ever assembled against them caved in. The Fijian forwards ran and handled like three-quarters, while their backs flattened opponents with tackles that back-row players would have been proud to execute. One of the most complete exhibitions of rugby football ever witnessed in Britain was the verdict of the press on this performance by 'The Ladies from Hell.'

Just to put their performance into perspective, more than half of the Barbarian side that October Saturday in 1970 became members of the 1971 Lions touring team which was the only side to date to take a series from the All Blacks in New Zealand.

THE GREATEST CONVERSION
SINCE ST PAUL'S

MURRAYFIELD, FEBRUARY 1971

The most pulsating match in Five Nations history was the Scotland-Wales clash at Murrayfield in 1971. A confident Welsh side that had annihilated England a fortnight earlier travelled north with nearly 20,000 of their fanatical supporters to meet a Scotland side that had fallen to a 13–8 defeat against France in Paris on the opening Saturday of the season.

The match took place in perfect conditions and the lead changed hands five times – three times in eight minutes during one stage of the second half – before, with Scotland ahead 18–14 with only a couple of minutes to go, Barry John opened the doors of the last-chance saloon by scrambling the ball into touch on the old grandstand side of the ground inside the Scottish 25.

With all Wales willing Delme Thomas, their lock, to lift his tired body for one last leap of the afternoon, the Llanelli linesman did his stuff admirably to intercept the Scottish throw and palmed the ball down to Gareth Edwards.

Out the ball went from Edwards and across the Welsh back division to Gerald Davies, who arced outside the defence for a wonderful try. The Scots did, however, manage to keep him hemmed in to the corner of the field, so that at 17–18 behind, Wales still needed the difficult conversion points to regain the lead. John Taylor, the London Welsh flanker, was entrusted with the all-important conversion and to maximise the angle took the ball out fully 35 yards before lining up his sights.

As the crowd on the old Murrayfield terraces waited in silence, Taylor took his measured run up and slammed the ball with his left foot. It sailed high and true between the posts: the most famous conversion since St Paul's on the Damascus road nearly 1900 years earlier.

Gordon Ross, a well known freelance, waxed lyrical. 'Never, in the history of rugby football, will any man, woman or child who was caught in the emotions of this magnificent and nail-bitingly exciting game, ever forget it,' he reported in the *Playfair Rugby Football Annual*'s review of the season.

THE WINNER WHO MISSED SEVEN PENALTIES

LLANELLI, MARCH 1971

The round-the-corner style favoured by virtually all modern place-kickers was not always so universally popular. True, rugby football always contained a handful of players who used the instep to kick. Nim Hall, the St Mary's Hospital, Richmond and England rugby player of the immediate post-war decade, for instance, was a well-known and successful soccer style kicker in an era when probably 95 per cent of goals were achieved with the more traditional straight on run-up, where the ball is being propelled by the kicker's toe. Ken Scotland, of Scotland, a decade after Hall, also landed goals with the soccer-style kick, most notably for the 1959 Lions in New Zealand.

But the player who more than any other was responsible for the spread in the round-the-corner method in modern rugby was a young Cardiff College of Education full-back named Robin Williams, who burst onto the first-class scene in the autumn of 1969. He turned out for Gwent against the Springboks that year and using his instep kicked goals with each foot to help the Welsh outfit to an unexpected 14–8 victory. By the following season the approach had become widespread in international rugby and nowadays it is rare to see a place kick taken any other way.

Robin Williams was unlucky to enter Welsh rugby a season after J P R Williams had taken out the long lease on the Number 15 jersey in the national side. Even so, the Cardiff student did represent Wales B and enjoyed mixed fortunes as a

232

kicker at that level.

In 1971 at Llanelli, he won the match for the Wales B side against their French counterparts. During the course of the game, though, he missed one, two, three . . . a staggering seven penalty kicks at goal. Admittedly, there was a tricky wind to contend with, but it was not until the dying moments that he found his kicking boots. With his trademark curling kick he edged his side 10–9 in front with a touchline conversion before sealing the win with his first successful penalty (his eighth attempt) with the last kick of the match.

DOCTOR DOUG SMITH'S CRYSTAL BALL

AUCKLAND, AUGUST 1971

The Lions of 1971 trod new ground. Never before (nor since) had a British/Irish combination returned victorious from a Test tour of New Zealand. But, with a back division of unsurpassed brilliance, in which every player was a master of the game's basic skills, and a forward unit that was both physically and tactically a match for the All Blacks, the Lions managed to pull off a famous triumph.

The credit for the side's technical expertise went to Carwyn James, the Lions' coach from Llanelli. James allowed a wealth of different talents to mature into a team that admitted the free expression of genius within the carefully prepared match plans drawn up for each new challenge. James simply created a side that was dedicated to winning and was devoted to its coach.

Then there was Dr Doug Smith who led the tour's senior management. A Lion himself in 1950, he was the charismatic manager who guided the brilliant class of '71. In all walks of life, one of the hallmarks of successful managers is the ability to make the task challenging for their charges while easing the routine chores behind the scenes. Dr Smith was the perfect leader in this respect, effectively and efficiently smoothing the path the players trod on tour.

But what really amazed the Lions and All Blacks alike was Smith's crystal-ball gazing. He confidently predicted at the outset of the visit that the Lions would return winners of the series, forecasting a 2–1 margin with one Test drawn. Bearing

234

in mind that no Lions side had ever succeeded in New Zealand and that in international rugby draws occur perhaps once in every 20 matches or so, this was a highly unlikely outcome.

Well, the Lions did win two Tests and were therefore already sure of a share of the series when they travelled to Auckland 2–1 up for the fourth and final Test in mid-August. That final Test went to the wire. It was 8–8 at the interval before Barry John nosed the Lions ahead with a penalty three minutes into the second half. Next, Bryan Williams made a searing break which led to an equalising New Zealand try scored by Tom Lister before J P R Williams, with an extraordinary dropped goal from 45 yards, restored the Lions' lead. Eight minutes from time, Laurie Mains kicked a penalty and, at 14–14, the match finished all square and the most extraordinary prediction in rugby history had come true.

THE GAME THAT NEVER WAS

DUBLIN, MARCH 1972

Saturday 11 March should have been a unique day in the history of the Five Nations Championship. It should have been the day when two unbeaten sides, Ireland and Wales, played at Lansdowne Road for the Triple Crown. Alas, owing to the intensity of the political troubles in the wake of the tragic Bloody Sunday events in Ireland, the match was cancelled. Never before nor since have the two nations had the chance to meet in Dublin with so much at stake.

Wales had won the Grand Slam in 1971 and provided the hugely successful Lions of that year with the largest contingent from the four Home Unions. The men in red began their 1972 Five Nations campaign with a hard-earned 12–3 victory at Twickenham, before smashing Scotland 35–12 at Cardiff to set up the possibility of a second successive Triple Crown.

Ireland, who had a fair sprinkling of the 1971 Lions' Test XV themselves, certainly did not lack experience either: Tom Kiernan, Kevin Flynn, Mike Gibson, Ray McLoughlin and Willie-John McBride collectively brought more than 48 seasons of international rugby into the Irish side that opened the Championship with a brave 14–9 win at Stade Colombes against France. Flynn, who had made his international debut in 1959, then snatched victory (16–12) from the jaws of defeat with a classical threequarter try in the dying moments of Ireland's game against England at Twickenham, to give his side distinct hopes of a first Grand Slam for 24 years.

That Twickenham win was on 12 February, but within a

236

week the Scottish Rugby Union had announced that, after carefully considering the relevant factors, they would not send a team to Dublin for the proposed international on 26 February. Possibly a critical factor in the decision was that their wing Billy Steele and hooker Robbie Clark were British servicemen. The Scots offered to play the match on a neutral ground, the French authorities promised to make Stade Colombes available, and there was even an approach from the Belgian Rugby Union to play the match in Brussels. But the Irish were adamant: they wanted the match to be staged in Dublin.

The decision was met more with sorrow than anger in Ireland. 'A bitter disappointment,' said Tom Kiernan, the Irish captain. Rugby more than any other recreation unites all of Ireland and the Ulstermen in the national side that season had all indicated that they were prepared to appear in Dublin. Sarsfield Hogan, a respected Irish Rugby Union official, recalled that in 1921 Scotland had fulfilled their fixture at Lansdowne Road on the same weekend as the Custom House was burnt down in Dublin, when the Troubles had previously reached a height.

Fears then began to grow that the Welsh would be influenced by the Scots' decision and cry off. The Welsh hooker, Jeff Young, an education officer in the RAF, made it perfectly clear to the Welsh Rugby Union that he had every intention of playing in the match if selected. But after the Welsh Rugby Union, Welsh players and clubs had received threatening letters purporting to have come from the IRA, the decision was made that Wales would not travel to Dublin. Moreover, two of the Welsh squad, Gerald Davies and Barry Llewelyn, had notified the Union that they did not wish to be considered were the Dublin match to go ahead.

And so one of the saddest chapters in the story of the Five Nations came to its close with the biggest disappointment felt by the Irish themselves. The following season, with the political situation still delicately balanced, England took the decision to fulfil the Dublin fixture, putting their faith in the Irish authorities' guarantees of safety, and John Pullin gained one of Lansdowne Road's biggest standing ovations when he led his England XV on to the pitch for that match. After suffering a 9–18 defeat, he memorably commented: 'We might not be much good, but at least we turn up.'

ENGLISH RUGBY'S FIRST CUP FINAL

TWICKENHAM, APRIL 1972

For more than a century after its foundation in 1871, the Rugby Football Union (RFU) steadfastly rejected all manner of proposals for making the game in England more competitive. National leagues or knockout cups, it was argued, were not in the best interests of the game.

It was in the year after the Union celebrated its centenary that a pilot scheme was adopted to launch an RFU Cup competition for senior clubs. There were difficulties. Squabbles regarding venues, kick-off times and even dates for arranging matches took some of the gloss off the inaugural event. On the plus side, however, the Cup ties brought together top sides who had never previously met and gave the club season a distinct climax. By the time that Gloucester and Moseley reached Twickenham for that first final in April 1972, the idea was embraced as a resounding success.

A crowd of 15,000 – a far cry from the 70,000 full houses that would follow in the 1990s – turned up to witness the novelty of a Cup Final for the senior English rugby clubs. Gloucester, after coming through the more difficult half of the draw in which they defeated Bath, Bristol, London Welsh and Coventry, were deserving winners of that first final, beating Moseley 17–6, though it was only with a flurry of scores in the dying minutes of the match that they consolidated their victory.

The sole blot on the day was that Ron Lewis, the only Welsh

referee who has controlled an RFU Cup final, had to dismiss Moseley's England lock, Nigel Horton, for punching. It was the first time for nearly fifty years that a player had been ordered off on a big Twickenham occasion.

SPRINGBOKS HUMILIATED

JOHANNESBURG, JUNE 1972

Imagine Manchester United playing Chester at the end of the 1999–2000 season. The premiership leaders against the basement of Division Three. Consider, too, Chester's chances of winning if the match were staged at Old Trafford. Impossible. No doubt about the result.

Yet in 1972, the rugby equivalent of just such a meeting was played out in Johannesburg's Ellis Park stadium when England toured the Republic at the end of a Five Nations season in which they had picked up the Wooden Spoon and had been whitewashed – losing all four matches – for the first time ever.

The last match of their tour was against the Springboks, the unofficial world champions. The South Africans had won seven and drawn two of their ten previous Tests. The run had included series victories over their toughest rivals – the All Blacks, France and the Wallabies. They had also drawn with Wales at Cardiff in 1970. Surely they would have little difficulty overcoming the challenge of an inferior England side?

What a surprise, then, when in front of 77,400 baying Afrikaaners, England's forwards led by John Pullin, the Bristol hooker, proceeded to master their mighty opponents, while the England halves exercised a strong tactical hold on the development of the game. The visitors' threequarters, too, played their part in tackling the South Africans out of the match while, behind them all, the late, great Sam Doble at full-back was a model of steadiness on his England debut.

It was Doble who kept England in the hunt in the first half.

241

Twice he brought them back on level terms with penalty goals after the hosts had gone ahead and his third kick, before half-time, gave England a 9–6 lead going into the interval.

England played with supreme confidence after the break. Jan Webster had proved a constant thorn in the flesh of the Springboks and it was no surprise when, two minutes into the second half, he paved the way to the only try of the afternoon. He pumped up a high kick and was the first player to arrive when Ray Carlson, the South African full-back, attempted to field it. Webster harried Carlson into making an error and gathered the loose ball to send Alan Morley in for a try. Doble converted and kicked a penalty to make it 18–6 before South Africa gained three consolation penalty points late in the game.

It was a totally unexpected victory.

A QUINTUPLE TIE

DUBLIN, APRIL 1973

The Five Nations tournament was first completed in 1910 and for most of the rest of the twentieth century dominated the rugby calendar in the northern hemisphere. The competition, with its unique atmosphere, was the envy of the three major southern hemisphere nations who had no major competition of their own until the successful Tri Nations was launched in 1996.

The pattern of fixtures in the Five Nations was more or less the same, year in year out, until 1974. The season invariably kicked off with Scotland meeting France on the second Saturday in January, followed by the England-Wales clash a week later, Wales and Scotland on the first Saturday of February and the Calcutta Cup on the third in March, and so on.

Down the years there were many requests for a change to the sequence. England and Wales, for instance, often endured the worst weather conditions of the year in January. Why couldn't they take their turn to play in dry conditions in March or April, it was argued. Indeed, when fixture congestion caused by having to accommodate overseas touring sides into the international schedule occurred, the Anglo-Welsh match was notably rearranged for late season in 1967 and 1970.

At length, the Five Nations committee decided to launch a ten-year rotation of fixtures featuring five Saturdays of double headers at fortnightly intervals. The experiment was such a success that it has been in operation now for nearly 30 years:

the younger generation of rugby followers can hardly imagine the Championship being arranged any differently.

But the last season under the old order provided an exciting climax that in turn resulted in a unique Five Nations outcome. The first nine matches of the 1973 campaign were won by the nation playing at home. The last match of the tournament was the Dublin meeting between Ireland and France. A win or even a draw for the French would give them the Five Nations title. A win by Ireland would bring perfect symmetry to the season, despite the fact that the odds against such an outcome at the outset of the campaign would have been more than a thousand to one.

Ireland led 6–0 after three minutes of the second half but then had to withstand a period of intense pressure as the French went all out for victory. Jean-Pierre Romeu, France's ace place kicker, went close with a couple of kickable penalty goals, and when Jean-François Philiponeau crossed for a try in the seventy-ninth minute of the match there was still a chance that France could draw and thus take the title. It all depended on Romeu landing the conversion. But he hooked his kick to leave the Five Nations with an unprecedented five-way share of the honours.

ACTRESSES AGAINST MODELS

SUNBURY-ON-THAMES, SEPTEMBER 1974

The women's game is now very much a part of modern rugby. There is a thriving club scene in England and Wales, an annual Five Nations Championship and even a well-organised four-yearly World Cup.

But things weren't always so structured in the women's game nor was it even accepted and taken seriously. As recently as 1974 the only women's matches likely to take place were charity games. One such game, staged at the ground of London Irish, featured a team of models against a team of actresses.

The coverage of the match deplored the lack of rough stuff and with sexist overtones reported: 'There was always the mirror. They stood in front of it at half-time repairing the damage to their carefully-prepared make-up.'

To add to the novelty of the occasion the girls played with two rugby footballs in the second half. 'It gave the fans two beautiful contests for the price of one,' it was recorded. Final score: Actresses 10; Models 10.

UP YOUR JUMPER

SYDNEY, MAY 1975

The late Daryl Haberecht was one of Australia's most gifted and innovative coaches. Apart from studying the Union game in great depth he was a keen observer of both League and American grid-iron tactics, and was not averse to pinching ideas from other codes that could be usefully tried in the Union game.

He achieved notoriety in May 1975 when, as the coach of the New South Wales Country XV, one of his well-rehearsed tricks led to a sensational last-minute win over arch-rivals Sydney. The score was 20–16 to the city slickers with time running out when the Country XV were awarded a penalty 40 metres from the Sydney goal-line.

John Hipwell, the Country XV's skipper, a veteran Test scrum-half and also Australia's captain at the time, was preparing to take a tap penalty when the Sydney side were confused by about a dozen of their opponents lining up shoulder to shoulder in a shallow crescent and with their backs to them. Hipwell was at the focus of the crescent and took the tap whereupon the ball was handed pass-the-parcel fashion along the line of players. The attackers further bewildered the Sydney players by making dummy movements as if handling the ball.

At Hipwell's signal every member of his team appeared to tuck arms under his jumper, turn and run in different directions towards the Sydney line. One of the players, Greg Cornelsen, actually did stuff the ball under his shirt but after running for ten to fifteen metres realised that he would have to hold it properly.

Even so, the trick had its desired effect, causing mass confusion in the Sydney ranks as defenders wondered who had possession of the ball. They eventually picked up Cornelsen, the big Country Number Eight, galloping towards them. Though challenged, the forward managed to make 30 metres before passing to Geoff Shaw who sent lock Brian Mansfield over near the posts. Referee Bob Fordham allowed the try and Country's fly-half, Jim Hindmarsh, landed the easy conversion to win the match 22–20.

Several sides tried to mimic the move in the weeks that followed before Australian referees referred the matter to the International Board, who ruled that the up-your-jumper tactic was against the spirit of the game and was therefore illegal.

Haberecht himself went from strength to strength. Within a couple of weeks of his side's infamous trick he masterminded their 14–13 win over Tony Neary's England touring team, and three years later he became Australia's coach. Taking the Wallabies to New Zealand in 1978, he unveiled a number of new tricks on tour, one of which was a variation on the up-your-jumper ruse. In the Test at Christchurch, John Hipwell arranged his team in a crescent at a tap penalty and feinted to pass. Simultaneously, his 14 colleagues began sprinting in different directions to confuse the All Blacks. Among the coach's other tricks was the 12–man scrum, while a more dangerous move involved the fly-half running up and over the backs of the forwards at a scrum. Sadly, Haberecht's national appointment was cut short owing to his ill-health.

UNDERWATER RUGBY

AUCKLAND, JUNE 1975

The worst pitch conditions under which a major Test match has been staged occurred in June 1975 in Auckland, where Scotland were due to play the All Blacks in the last match of their short tour. It was the only international of the visit and the Scots were booked to fly home the next day.

Early in the morning of the match torrential rain began to fall in Auckland. Twelve hours later it was still bucketing down when Scotland and New Zealand (wearing white shirts to avoid a clash for monochrome television viewers) marched on to an Eden Park ground that was covered by large pools of water. Meteorologists estimated that nearly ten centimetres had fallen prior to kick-off time. The water lay so deep around the playing area that sections of the goal lines and touchlines were obscured and during the match the ball frequently deceived players who overran it as it stopped dead on the sodden ground. One of the in-goal areas and a large part of the playing field bordering it was such a lake that the ball became submerged when kicked ahead into that area.

Before and during the match an army of firemen pumped water away from the playing surface and the walkways that gave spectators access to the stands. Planks had to be supplied to help those who had tickets for the covered stand to reach their reserved seats.

Pure commercial pressure led to the match taking place. More than £85,000 had been taken from ticket sales to 55,000 spectators beforehand, and with the Scots flying out the next

248

day there was clearly no prospect of re-arranging the Test. As it was, 45,000 braved the elements to see one of the strangest matches of all time.

There was no holding the All Blacks once the match started. They adopted the perfect tactical approach: get the ball, kick it high ahead and wait for the opposition to make mistakes. Their intentions were made clear in the third minute when Bruce Hay, on his Test debut for Scotland, was flattened gathering a high kick. Hay broke his arm and was back in the dressing room within five minutes of the kick-off. Soon after, in a splash of spray, Joe Karam was adding the first of four successful conversions, turning Hamish Macdonald's try into a goal.

Sid Going took a tight tactical grip on the match and, revelling in the conditions behind the sub-aqua experts in his pack, he was the catalyst of the All Blacks' three remaining tries. The final result was 24–0 to New Zealand, who hardly dropped a pass all afternoon. It was a fair reflection of the play in this peculiar match, but under normal circumstances the game would surely have been postponed. 'As foul a day as one could possibly conceive,' said Vivian Jenkins in his report for the *Sunday Times*, adding: 'only in New Zealand could so many apparent lunatics have put in an appearance, in spite of everything.'

THE REFEREE WHO FORGOT THE LAWS

MURRAYFIELD, JANUARY 1976

A refereeing error that may have changed the course of the match occurred at Murrayfield in January 1976 when Scotland played France on the opening Saturday of the season's Five Nations championship. The game was played on a wind-swept ground where place-kicking became a lottery.

Scotland opened the scoring when Dougie Morgan, their scrum-half, dropped a neat goal. After that the match became a battle of the kickers as both sides tried to score through penalty goals. Andy Irvine missed with a long-range effort before sending his next ball high over the posts to give Scotland what everyone believed would be a 6–0 lead. The Scots were sitting on a ten-match unbeaten record at Murrayfield and the crowd felt at this stage that the eleventh win of the sequence was in the bag. But to their dismay they realised that the English referee, Ken Pattinson, had disallowed the goal.

Because of the strong wind, Irvine had requested the help of a ball holder. Prop Ian McLauchlan offered his assistance and placed the ball for the successful kick, but in order to accommodate his kicker's round-the-corner style he had to lie in front of the ball to hold it. The referee ruled that McLauchlan was, therefore, offside at the time of the kick and ordered a scrum. It was a mistake. The laws of the game at this time clearly stated that in such circumstances the placer could be in front of the kicker.

Scotland eventually went down 13–6 to the French, but

arguments raged over a decision that Mr Pattinson was man enough to admit was an error. Scotland felt that the 6–0 lead that the award of the penalty would have given them would have helped to lift their game. Poor Mr Pattinson never again took control of a major international match.

HADEN WINS AN OSCAR

CARDIFF, NOVEMBER 1978

For moments of high drama, the Test series between Wales and New Zealand takes some beating. The outcome of the first match in 1905 hinged on a controversial refereeing decision, in 1935 Wales snatched a one-point victory with a dramatic late try and in 1953 it was an inspired Clem Thomas cross-kick that paved the way for another desperate late win when Ken Jones snaffled up a lucky bounce to score a late try. Notably, Wales won all those matches.

The boot was on the other foot, though, when the sides met at Cardiff in 1978. That was the last time in the series that Wales fielded a side that could really hold a candle to the All Blacks. The Welsh began with considerable promise and led 9–0 after 24 minutes, before New Zealand pulled back a try when Stu Wilson followed a chip ahead by Bill Osborne and won a race to the south-east corner for a try. The same Osborne, however, committed a late tackle moments later and Gareth Davies kicked Wales into a 12–4 lead which, on the run of play up to that time, they thoroughly deserved.

New Zealand had suffered a blow in the ninth minute when Clive Currie, their full-back, fractured his jaw in a heavy tackle by Steve Fenwick. On came Brian McKechnie, who had only found himself promoted to the New Zealand bench on the morning of the match. Two minutes before half time he landed a simple penalty to make the score 12–7 at the break.

Up to this point the Welsh forwards had dominated the set pieces with the Welsh lineout experts, Geoff Wheel and Allan

Martin, particularly productive. Wales continued to rule the roost but began committing careless errors, McKechnie narrowing the deficit to only two points when the home backs were caught encroaching at a lineout near their own 25.

As the game moved towards its climax, the All Blacks forced a lineout on the south side of the ground and just outside the Welsh 25. The atmosphere in the ground was electric as Bobby Windsor prepared to throw in for Wales. He lined up Geoff Wheel standing at the front of the line and placed the ball perfectly for the agile Swansea lock to pluck it from the air.

In jumping for the ball, however, Wheel appeared to put his left hand on the shoulder of Frank Oliver, his opponent, and referee Roger Quittenton immediately whistled for a penalty, assuming that the Welshman had been levering. Number 19, Brian McKechnie, stepped forward to calmly stroke the ball between the posts and give New Zealand the 13–12 lead that they held for the remaining two minutes of the match.

Many in the crowd and press box had watched that lineout closely. Both Oliver and his lock partner Andy Haden, who was standing behind him to mark the other Welsh lineout threat, Allan Martin, had recoiled from the lineout with unnatural speed. They had not, it seemed, attempted to contest the set-piece. Instead, their plan had been to inveigle the referee into thinking that they had been shoved out of the line in order to win a penalty.

The Welsh media were incensed by these acts of pure games-manship. Haden should have been given an Oscar said some; pure Hollywood was the reaction of others. The supporting cast of referee Mr Quittenton and the Welsh forwards were eagerly watched on video footage. In the trial by television that followed, there was incontrovertible evidence that Wheel's inner hand had come into contact with Oliver's shoulder, vindicating the referee's decision. But there was also no doubt that Haden and Oliver had dived.

The Welsh national newspaper, the *Western Mail*, carried the story on its front page on the Monday after the match. Geoff Wheel confirmed that the two had dived while former Welsh captain, Clem Thomas, who was himself a journalist, made no bones about the matter: 'They were cheating,' he said. 'The referee was conned.' Russell Thomas, the All Blacks' manager, paid tribute to the refereeing but refused to be drawn into a row over the incident.

THE PRINTER'S NIGHTMARE

PARIS, MARCH 1980

Colm Tucker was a typical all-action Munster flanker who had the misfortune to arrive on the Irish Test scene while Fergus Slattery was an automatic choice on their back-row. Tucker's dynamic play was first noted by the wider rugby audience of the Home Unions when, in 1978, he was a member of the famous Munster XV that defeated New Zealand 12–0. He battled with an insuperable will to win and his determination eventually carried him into the Irish side for a couple of Five Nations appearances in 1979. A year later he became the first Shannon player to win selection for the Lions.

From an early time he had to accept calmly that some of the less enlightened copy takers on British newspapers would report his name inaccurately. No doubt he became used to seeing his first name appear as Colin in the English press reports of his matches.

Even he, though, must have raised an eyebrow when he opened the programme for the 1980 France-Ireland match in Paris. Nominated as one of the Ireland pack replacements for the match, he saw that his surname had been unwittingly misprinted by the French programme editors. The letter T was replaced with the letter F . . . and so a proof-reader's nightmare became a programme collector's treasured item.

Mid-way through the first half he came on to replace John O'Driscoll on the side of the scrum. The unsuspecting French announcer heralded the substitute by referring to the programme and using 'that word', very much to the amusement of the Irish contingent in the crowd.

NEARLY SENT OFF

LLANELLI, OCTOBER 1980

Rugby relations between Wales and New Zealand cooled considerably during the 1970s. An incident at the Angel Hotel in Cardiff in 1972 after the All Blacks' 19–16 win in the international resulted in the sending home of Keith Murdoch, New Zealand's prop. Then, in 1978, the Andy Haden dive when New Zealand snatched a late one-point win against Wales, together with a nasty stamping incident in which J P R Williams received seven stitches during Bridgend's club match against the All Blacks, combined to leave an unfortunate taste.

It was in the spirit of *glasnost* that New Zealand were invited to Wales for a five-match tour to help celebrate the Welsh Rugby Union's centenary in 1980. The move was seen as a welcome hand to an old adversary that had frankly been growing steadily stronger than the Welsh since the 1960s. But the New Zealanders were honoured to accept the invitation and played open, attractive rugby under the captaincy of Graham Mourie during their month in Wales.

So positive were the feelings among guest and host that in the Llanelli match at Stradey Park a potential controversy was probably defused by the reactions of three seasoned Welsh international players. The Scarlets, famous 9–3 winners against the Sixth All Blacks of 1972, gave Mourie's men their stiffest test of the centenary tour and after leading 10–3 at the interval, breweries all over Wales were again praying that the Llanelli celebrants would drink their hostelries dry. But hopes of another night of Scarlet fever were dashed by a second half

New Zealand rally that resulted in a 16–10 win for the visitors.

The moment that threatened to throw the tour into turmoil came at the end of the playing time when New Zealand lock Graeme Higginson was allegedly caught stamping in a ruck. The referee was the experienced Scot, Allan Hosie, and after taking advice from a touch judge he called the New Zealand captain over. By this stage the large crowd was shouting, 'off, off'.

After an earnest discussion with Mourie in the presence of Higginson, Mr Hosie stretched out his right arm and appeared to make a dismissal gesture with his open left palm. Mourie's body language, moreover, bore the resignation of a captain witnessing one of his players receiving his marching orders. 'Off he'll go in my estimation,' was Gareth Edwards's reaction on BBC Wales television's broadcast of the match.

There then followed an extraordinary commotion as Llanelli fly half Phil Bennett ran up to Mr Hosie and engaged him in an animated conversation. At times Bennett was so agitated that both his feet were off the ground. The Llanelli skipper Ray Gravell and veteran Welsh cap Derek Quinnell joined Bennett before Mr Hosie drew a conclusion to matters by blowing for the end of the game.

The incident dominated the press reports of the match. The three Welshmen, Mourie and Mr Hosie all spoke afterwards of how Higginson had received a stern warning to the effect that he would be off next time if he perpetrated a stamping offence. But the story was received with suspicion and the feeling that prevailed was that the Welsh players, anxious that the tour should not be wrecked, had talked Mr Hosie out of sending a player off.

A TRY AWARDED IN ERROR

TWICKENHAM, MARCH 1981

France came to Twickenham in search of their third Grand Slam on the last Saturday of the 1981 Five Nations Championship. They were rather lucky to secure the title, a refereeing error enabling them to score a converted try that contributed to their winning margin.

There was a gale-force wind blowing when France won the toss and elected to make first use of it. Their fly-half, Guy Laporte, was the first to score with a long range dropped goal. Soon afterwards came the illegal move.

A quick throw-in on the England 22 resulted in Jean-Pierre Rives creating the space for his fellow flanker Pierre Lacans to canter over to the left of the posts for a try that Laporte converted into a 9–0 French lead. The try was awarded in error because the ball which Pierre Berbizier had used for the throw was supplied by a bystander. This contravened the relevant law, which stated that for a quick throw in the ball that went into touch must be used, that it must be handled only by the players and that it must be thrown in correctly.

The match, otherwise controlled with characteristic quiet authority by Allan Hosie, the respected Scottish referee, finished in a 16–12 win for France.

FLOUR BOMBS INTERRUPT PLAY

AUCKLAND, SEPTEMBER 1981

It was the oddest tour ever undertaken by the Springboks. Anti-apartheid demonstrations during their visit to New Zealand meant that the tourists were kept under strict security for the best part of six weeks. At times the Springboks were unable to leave their hotel rooms and there were occasions when late changes of plan necessitated their sleeping on sports-hall floors. At every match venue they had to run the gauntlet of protesters to fulfil their fixtures.

Two of the games were cancelled. At Hamilton, in the first week of the tour, more than 200 demonstrators ripped down a chain fence to break on to the pitch where they sprinkled tacks and staged a sit-in on half-way. The sides had changed and tossed for ends and a crowd of 25,000 was in place to see the Springboks take on Waikato. But the protesters defied the attempts of the police to disperse them and after an hour it was reluctantly decided by the organisers that the match should be cancelled. Thereafter, barbed wire and batons were the order of the day at all of the Springboks' matches. But even this was not enough to allay the fears of the rugby authorities at Timaru where, anticipating a demonstration that they would not be able to handle, the rugby authorities cancelled the South Canterbury game.

Nevertheless, against such a grim and stifling backdrop, the tourists managed to maintain their cool and played some skilful rugby. They were unbeaten in their provincial matches and went into the third and final Test at Auckland with the series delicately balanced at one win apiece. Their star player was Naas Botha, whose kicking throughout the tour was a revelation. The fair-haired fly-half finished with 129 points from eight tour appearances in New Zealand, an impressive average of just over 16 a match.

The most bizarre game of this most bizarre tour was the final Test – the series decider in Auckland. During the match a Cessna aircraft constantly strafed the pitch with flour bombs, flares and leaflets. The plane passed so low at times that there were fears that it might crash and in one of its missions the All Black prop Gary Knight was temporarily stunned by a flour bomb. But both captains insisted on referee Clive Norling of Wales allowing the game to run its course and the highest moment of rugby drama of the entire tour came in the final moments of time added on for stoppages. Allan Hewson, the New Zealand full-back, kicked a long range penalty to win the Test 25–22 and wrap up the series.

'There will probably never be another Test match like this,' wrote the New Zealand rugby historians Rod Chester and Nev McMillan. 'The tension generated by the closeness and importance of the game, combined with the efforts of protesters inside, outside and above the ground, made for an exhilarating and yet terrifying afternoon.'

THE MOST FAMOUS STREAKER OF
THEM ALL

TWICKENHAM, JANUARY 1982

The streaking phenomenon began among American college students in the 1970s, but the first streaker to bare all in front of thousands at a sporting event was Michael O'Brien at Twickenham during the 1974 England-Wales rugby match. He started the craze for stripping off at big sporting occasions and was famously captured on photographic film, a Christ-like figure being frog-marched along Twickenham's east touchline by local bobby, PC Perry, who had thoughtfully removed his helmet to cover young O'Brien's embarrassment.

O'Brien, who is now a respectable stockbroker living in Australia, was swiftly removed to Twickenham police station where he was charged and released. According to legend, he managed to get back into the ground to see the last 20 minutes of England's first victory over the Welsh for eleven years.

The most famous streak and certainly the most publicised one came at the same ground during an England-Australia match nearly eight years after O'Brien's pioneering effort. Erika Roe, a 24–year-old who worked for an art dealer in Petersfield, thoughtfully waited until half-time during a tense match to make her eye-catching appearance in front of the packed south stand on a day early in the New Year. 'I didn't want to interrupt the game – I wanted to watch it,' she explained to an interviewer later.

The media had a field day. 'Titters at Twickers,' it was revealed in one tabloid, while the game's bible, the *Rothmans*

Rugby Yearbook, referred to a highlight of the season being 'when a lady named Erika erupted on to the field like a galleon in full sail, but minus her spinnakers.'

But perhaps the best comment of all came from one of the England players who was temporarily distracted from the captain's pep-talk during Ms Roe's half-time interlude. Bill Beaumont was the England skipper at the time and his side were only 6–3 ahead with the wind to face after the break. The result was far from a foregone conclusion and Bill was earnestly trying to rally his troops for a big effort in the second half when he realised no-one was listening to him. 'What's the problem?' he asked. 'Everyone's watching a girl over there who seems to have your bum on her chest, Bill,' came the reply.

Erika's display inspired England to great heights in the second half as they ran out 15–11 winners.

ALPHABET SOUP

TWICKENHAM, APRIL 1983

In the early years of the game, identifying players posed a big problem for spectators. Although programmes listing teams have been part and parcel of rugby since the 1870s, jersey numbering as an aid to identification was not introduced until the early 1900s. The first international match to feature numbered teams was probably the famous Wales–New Zealand clash of 1905, though it was not until 1922, when Wales and England met at Cardiff, that both sides first wore numbers in a Five Nations game.

The Scots were the last to adopt the practice of identification, but by the 1930s it was common for teams to be labelled in all big matches. Even then, however, there was no systematic approach to the allocation of labels to positions. Some sides numbered from one to fifteen starting with the full-back and working through the side to the forwards, while others started with the halves or even with the back row. In the late 1920s, Wales even refused to issue a number 13 jersey for superstitious reasons – not that they ever seemed to win during a decade of rugby disasters for the principality. They then completely and inexplicably abandoned numbers for letters in the 1930s, a practice that lasted for nearly 20 years until 1949 when a new red dye was adopted for the national shirts and they reverted to numbered jerseys.

So, the famous Welsh fly-half factory immortalised in song by Max Boyce that made 'number tens' for Wales, actually churned out Cliff Jones in the 1930s with the letter 'F' on his back and Cliff Morgan in the 1950s wearing number '6'. Then in 1967 the International Board legislated that the numbering of Test teams should be standardised according to a fashion that persists to this day. Therefore, David Watkins, Barry John and Phil Bennett were the first authentic fly-halves to wear the number '10' shirt for Wales.

Until rugby became professional, the clubs were allowed to use whatever system took their fancies – either letters or numbers. Bath, like the old Welsh teams, numbered from 1 to 16 leaving out number 13, while two of England's other major clubs, Bristol and Leicester, curiously settled for letters. What made the alphabet soup even more confusing when these two sides met was the fact that Bristol lettered from A to O starting from the full-back while Leicester labelled in the reverse order.

The most famous occasion on which the two clubs met in a life-sized game of Rugby Scrabble was in the John Player Cup final at Twickenham in 1983. Bristol beat Leicester 28–22 on a day when two of the best fly-halves in England, Stuart Barnes of Bristol and Les Cusworth of Leicester, wore jerseys lettered F and J respectively.

At least the professional era has ensured that English club matches are now played by teams that wear numbers that are meaningful to everyone.

THE RECORD SCORE

VERGT, NOVEMBER 1984

The *Monty Python* comedy team devised a famous sketch in the 1970s in which a Long John Silver XI played soccer against a spoof Watford Gynaecologists XI. The slapstick involved one team standing virtually stationary on crutches while the opposition, dressed in white coats, tore about the pitch scoring goal after goal.

It must have been a little bit like that watching the French third division club, Vergt, playing rugby in November 1984. They were beaten 236–0 by Gujah-Misters one week and succumbed by 350–0 to Lavardac seven days later, conceding 66 tries, thereby breaking all scoring records for all classes of rugby.

There was an explanation to these huge defeats. Vergt had recently had four of their players suspended and in protest offered merely passive resistance almost to the point of just standing on the pitch while fulfilling their fixtures.

A VERY PECULIAR SENDING OFF

LAUGHARNE, JANUARY 1988

Gerry 'Ginger' McLoughlin was a bulwark of the Ireland pack that won the Triple Crown and Championship in 1982. A man of tremendous strength, he provided the abiding memory of the famous win at Twickenham that year when, early in the second half, he led a raid for the corner from a maul in the English 22 and finished off scoring the only try of his Test career to set Ireland on course for a 16–15 victory.

He was a typical son of Munster, hailing from Limerick, and his shock of red hair made him stand out in even the most protracted scrum or maul. Never one to start trouble, he would be the first to admit that he was never an angel on the rugby pitch. Certainly he was well able to mix it with the best of them during a successful playing career that culminated in a Lions tour to New Zealand in 1983.

Long after his international career was over he took up a position as bar steward at the Gilfach Goch rugby club in Wales and frequently turned out for the first XV. He was a part of the side that enjoyed a run to the fourth round of the WRU Challenge Cup in 1988.

In the third round match of that campaign at Laugharne, he was involved in a very peculiar incident. An argy-bargy involving some of the front-row forwards at a lineout attracted the attention of Roy Rees, the referee. Ginger, never one to argue with authority but perhaps revealing his guilty conscience, heard the referee's comments and trudged quietly off the pitch to his early shower and thought nothing more about the incident.

267

Some 15 minutes or so later Mr Rees realised that Gilfach were a man short when a scrum went down minus a tight-head prop. It then dawned on everyone that Ginger had thought that he had been sent off and had left the field. Apparently, when he lectured the players for that bit of nonsense at the lineout Mr Rees had said sternly: 'Push off and let's get on with the game.' Ginger literally took 'push off' to be his marching orders.

Gilfach's 14 men won through all the same beating Laugharne 28–19.

CAMPO'S BIG BLUNDER

SYDNEY, JULY 1989

Arguably rugby's costliest error was perpetrated by one of the game's most sublime players: David Ian Campese, world record Test try scorer. Campo's moment of madness came at a crucial moment in the third Test tie-breaker between Australia and the Lions at the Sydney Football Stadium in July 1989.

The Lions had been well beaten in the first Test, before bouncing back to square the series with a 19–12 win in a second international that was controversial because of the rough tactics adopted by both sides.

For the final Test both sides put the boxing gloves away and played a clean, hard-fought game that went to the wire. The early exchanges were between the place-kickers, Gavin Hastings for the Lions and Michael Lynagh for Australia notching four penalties between them, as the visitors went 9–3 up. The next score was a try for Australia by Ian Williams, their wing, and Lynagh's conversion made it all square at 9–9 as the sides went into the interval.

The Lions were disappointed by this score. After all, they had won the greater share of the possession in the first half and their backs had shown more handling and running skill than their Wallaby counterparts. Australia's try, however, was a gem with Lynagh having tricked the Lions defence with a tantalising run that created the opening for Williams. And when the Australian fly-half put Australia in front with another penalty goal early in the second half, it looked as if the writing was on the wall for the tourists.

269

Then came the turning point of the series. Soon after the restart, Rob Andrew hoisted a high kick towards the Australian goal, forcing a scrum in the shadow of the posts. The Lions heeled and the England fly-half took a drop shot that went wide. Deep in goal, David Campese gathered the loose ball and all he had to do was touch down for safety. But Campese had other ideas. Instead he began to run it. Immediately Ieuan Evans, the Lions right wing, was up to close him down, and when challenged the Australian threw a feeble pass to his full-back, Greg Martin. To Martin's horror the ball went to ground and Evans, quick as a flash, pounced on it for the try that restored the Lions' lead, 13–12.

Two penalties each by Hastings and Lynagh left the Lions winners of the match by 19–18 and of the series by 2–1. All thanks to David Campese's big blunder.

AN ABANDONED INTERNATIONAL

COLORADO SPRINGS, JULY 1991

Although there have been several postponed Tests and even a handful of cancelled international matches down the years, there have been only two Tests that actually started but never finished.

In February 1885 at the Ormeau Grounds in Belfast, Ireland and Scotland played for thirty minutes in a storm before the match was abandoned. Scotland led by a try to nil when the sides retired and in the discussions that took place afterwards, it was decided that the score should stand unless a replay could be rearranged.

A replay was arranged and the sides met a fortnight later in Edinburgh where the Scots again held the upper hand, winning by the convincing margin of a goal and two tries to nil. At the time, the abandoned match was erased from the record books and both Unions recognised only the replayed match as having a place in the official log of the series. It was more than a hundred years later that the abandoned game was officially recognised and given retrospective Test status in both Ireland and Scotland.

The only other match to fall into the abandoned category took place during France's warm-up tour for the 1991 World Cup. They played four matches that summer in North America, including two Tests against the US Eagles. The second of the internationals, staged in Colorado Springs, started in a downpour and, when thunder and lightning came perilously close to the playing area, referee Albert Adams from

South Africa abandoned the match in the interest of safety. France were leading 10–3, Serge Blanco having scored the thirty-eighth and last Test try of his illustrious career, when Mr Adams called the game off at half time.

French minds, perhaps, went back to a tragic occasion in May 1976 when one of their talented international wings of the time, Jean-François Philiponeau, was struck by lightning and killed whilst playing in a friendly for his club, Montferrand. He was only 25 at the time.

THE WORLD CUP'S DEFINING MOMENT

CARDIFF, OCTOBER 1991

Momentum for a Rugby World Cup gathered pace during the early 1980s. Most of the drive for a world-wide tournament came from the southern hemisphere and was probably fuelled by their desire to have a formal competition that enabled the mighty Tri-nation powers to compare themselves. Less enthusiasm for the idea came from the European countries who, after all, had the Five Nations. By 1986, however, players everywhere were warming to the idea and a year later the inaugural competition was held in Australia and New Zealand.

There was no qualifying tournament for admission to that first World Cup. Sixteen nations took part by invitation and after a heady month of 32 international matches New Zealand beat France 29–9 in the first final, staged in Auckland. The tournament was such a resounding success that it quickly established itself as the focal point of the game. Membership of the International Board grew apace after that and qualifying rounds and seeding tournaments were held before the 1991 event which took place in Britain, Ireland and France.

As a result of the pre-tournament matches the only new-comers in 1991 were Western Samoa. In 1990 they had finished top of the Asian-Pacific qualifying group, defeating Japan, Korea and Tonga, and were thus seeded behind Australia, Wales and Argentina in the World Cup group based in Wales. No-one expected them to win a game, even though the Samoans were sitting on a 15-match unbeaten international record that stretched back to their defeat by Romania in Bucharest two years earlier.

Their eagerly awaited opening group match was on the first Sunday of the competition against Wales at Cardiff. It was the first time that Wales played a home international on a Sunday and it was to become the first time that one of the so-called minnow nations – those who were not among the Big Eight senior members of the International Board – beat a senior nation in the World Cup.

The Western Samoans triumphed 16–13, the match turning early in the second half when To'o Vaega scored a try following up a kick ahead. That was the score that launched a golden period of Samoan offence during which the Welsh were completely swept aside. With 25 minutes to go the Western Samoans were 13–3 ahead and as the Welsh spectators began whistling 'Always look on the bright side of life' somehow everyone present knew that they were witnessing a piece of rugby history.

Wales did restore some pride by scoring a late try, but the result meant that only the failures of others would enable them to reach their expected quarter final. 'Good job we didn't have to play the whole of Samoa,' said a disgruntled Welsh spectator as he made his way from the ground after the match.

The Samoans gave Australia, the eventual Cup winners, a tough game in pouring rain at Pontypool before going down 9–3, but their subsequent 35–12 win against Argentina at Sardis Road, Pontypridd, assured them of a quarter-final with Scotland and eliminated Wales from the final stages.

The darlings of the competition, the Samoans were finally knocked out at Murrayfield but still managed a joyous lap of honour for their handful of followers in Edinburgh and their thousands watching on a large screen out in the open and in the middle of the night back home in Apia. But it was that defeat of Wales at Cardiff that was the defining moment of World Cup history, showing that the old order could no longer be taken for granted.

FRENCH DISGRACE

PARIS, FEBRUARY 1992

Discipline in French rugby has often caused concern to the Home Unions. The watershed in the 1930s, when France were suspended from the Five Nations, had its roots in the rough, over-competitive play witnessed in the French club championship and there have been other occasions down the years when the French have come under the spotlight for rough play, most notably during the 1991–2 campaign.

Matters first came to a head that season in the France-England quarter-final in Paris during the Rugby World Cup. England were 19–10 winners of a hard, uncompromising match in which violence was always bubbling just below the surface of the scrums. The match, unfortunately, was soon overshadowed by events off the field. As the referee, David Bishop of New Zealand, was making his way to the dressing rooms Daniel Dubroca, the French coach, was observed grabbing Bishop by the collar in the tunnel. Only the quick intervention of Keith Lawrence, one of the touch judges, prevented a disgraceful incident turning uglier.

The upshot was that Dubroca was stripped of his post as French coach and Pierre Berbizier, the former scrum-half, was appointed to take over for the 1992 Five Nations Championship. Berbizier's arrival as coach was heralded amidst new French commitments to tighten discipline at all levels of the game. But once again, the match with England was to be marred by another disappointing chapter in French rugby history.

275

Two French players were sent off by Ireland's Stephen Hilditch during the second half of a match in which France were completely outplayed by an effective England outfit. Grégoire Lascubé was dismissed for stamping as the French pack, effectively subdued by their English superiors, finally snapped in the last quarter. He was followed to the sidelines by hooker Vincent Moscato, a member of an all-international club front-row at Bègles-Bordeaux, who was clearly seen head-butting an opponent.

In fairness to the French authorities they moved quickly to denounce the miscreants. Both men were suspended by the International Board for seven months and were never again selected to represent France.

TRY FROM THE END OF THE WORLD

AUCKLAND, JULY 1994

You have to hand it to the French: for manufacturing tries out of the blue they are unsurpassable. Witness that miraculous effort from their own dead-ball-line in the 1991 Grand Slam decider against England at Twickenham. It was the longest move leading up to a try in any Test match, yet sadly for France they lost the game.

The French produced a similar effort at Auckland in the second Test of their tour of New Zealand three years later. It, too, was a surprise move launched from a do-or-die position near the French line which then swept the length of the pitch. But the difference this time was that the try, which was one of the most remarkable tries in the annals of Test rugby, won the match for France.

France had never won a Test series against the All Blacks and only four visitors in nearly a century of combat had succeeded in taking a rubber in New Zealand before Philippe Saint André's side descended on Auckland for the final match of their tour. With 90 seconds of play remaining the French trailed 20–16 as Steve Bachop, New Zealand's fly half, attempted to push them back into their own 22 with a kick to touch. His kick missed its target but was gathered by Saint André, who with 13 of his colleagues in front of him, launched an ambitious counter-attack instead of kicking for touch.

He ran past three New Zealanders and made his way to his own ten-metre-line, where he was eventually overwhelmed by

All Black tackles. But the damage had been done. His run had made inroads into the defence and, more importantly, put the rest of his team into a position from which the attack could be continued. The French props then did their spadework and dug the ball out from the ruck, whereupon it passed through three more pairs of hands before Emile Ntamack stretched his legs and passed the ball on to Laurent Cabannes. The flanker combined with Yann Delaigue to turn the remaining All Black defence inside out and they worked Guy Accoceberry, moving diagonally to the left, clear for a run to the posts. Showing a quick turn of pace, New Zealand's full-back John Timu came speeding across to take the Frenchman, but Jean-Luc Sadourny had by now raced up outside Accoceberry and he was on hand to take the pass and slide over to the left of the posts for the try that won the match and with it the series.

'It was a try from the end of the world,' said a delighted and exhausted Saint André at the post match press conference. Everyone knew what he meant. It was the most sensational last-minute winning try in France's Test history to date.

LIGHTS GO OUT IN PORT ELIZABETH

PORT ELIZABETH, JUNE 1995

The Boet Erasmus Stadium in Port Elizabeth has had its share of difficult moments in its Test history. In 1963, in the final Test of that year's series between the Springboks and the Wallabies, the match erupted into a riot in the second half as bottles were thrown on to the pitch, cars were vandalised and policemen had to fire pistols into the air to quell demonstrators. The Australians, who understandably were more concerned for their own safety than with the play of the Springboks, wanted the referee to abandon the match. 'It was a complete shambles,' one of the Australian players was reported to have said, reflecting on the failure of officials to keep the crowd under control.

Thirty-two years later, during the Rugby World Cup, the Boet Erasmus administration had more nightmares, this time as a result of power failure. South Africa and Canada were due to meet one another at the ground in a pool match, but a floodlight failure delayed the start of the match by 40 minutes.

But by the end of the match, it was rugby football itself that plunged into darkness. A highly unsavoury incident late in the match was witnessed by millions of viewers around the world. Ten minutes from time a scuffle began near the touchline and turned into a huge brawl as several players from both sides became involved with fists and feet flying. It ended in the sending off of three players – two Canadians, Gareth Rees and Rod Snow, plus the Springboks' hooker, James Dalton. Dalton

279

thus missed the opportunity to play in the knockout stages that took his side to the final of the competition, as too did the winger Pieter Hendriks, who although not sent off at the time, was later cited for his part in the fracas and suspended accordingly.

The strange upshot was that South Africa were permitted to replace the players suspended from the squad, enabling them to introduce their ace threequarter Chester Williams, who had been unavailable through injury when the original squad for the competition had been named three weeks earlier.

THE LONGEST MATCH

JOHANNESBURG, JUNE 1995

The intense rivalry between South Africa and New Zealand dates from 1921 when the Springboks made their first visit to the land of the long black cloud. The series was drawn with each side winning one game with the third being drawn. The closeness of the Tests cemented a strong and lasting rugby bond between the two nations.

Until the advent of the Rugby World Cup in 1987, the two nations invariably and undisputedly laid claim to the unofficial title of world rugby champions. Sometimes it was South Africa that held the upper hand, most notably in 1937, 1949 and 1960. On other occasions, New Zealand were on top, as in 1956, 1965 and 1981.

Even during the apartheid years, when South Africa were starved of Tests against the so-called first-world nations of the International Board, a rebel New Zealand side undertook a tour of the Republic. That side, which toured in 1986 and was known as the Cavaliers, was referred to by the South Africans as All Blacks. The Springboks won the series 3–1 giving the players who appeared in the games their full national colours.

The Springboks were in sporting isolation when the 1987 and 1991 World Cups were won by New Zealand and Australia respectively. South Africans, however, steadfastly refused to acknowledge that any nation could possibly call itself world champions if the Springboks had not been a part of the World Cup. When apartheid was lifted in 1992 and South Africa returned to the sporting fold, they had three years to build a team to prove themselves at the next World Cup.

They did have the benefit of home advantage for the 1995 event in a draw that looked suspiciously as if it were designed to yield a New Zealand-South Africa final. Certainly both nations made it with little difficulty to the last four.

New Zealand's spectacular demolition of England in the second of the semi-finals was in stark contrast to the grit South Africa relied on to beat lively France. New Zealand were the most exciting team to watch in the tournament and consequently were installed as the narrow favourites before the final at Johannesburg's Ellis Park stadium.

Never before had there been a necessity for an international match to go into extra time, but after 80 minutes of power rugby between two well-matched sides the scores were all square at 9–9, neither side having managed to break the other's defence to score a try. English referee Ed Morrison gave the sides a much-needed breather before whistling for the start of the first additional period. Andrew Mehrtens nosed the All Blacks in front with a penalty in the first minute, but Joel Stransky levelled with a similar score in the last minute of the first period.

As the stalemate continued into the second period of extra time, spectators began to wonder whether the winners would be decided on disciplinary records. If the sides remained level on three penalties and a dropped goal apiece, the rules of the competition stated that the title would be settled in this way.

Then, with seven minutes to go, from a scrum on the New Zealand 22, Joel Stransky dropped the goal that secured the Rainbow Nation's World Cup win. International rugby had seen its longest match and skipper François Pienaar had led South Africa back to the top of world rugby. But it was the other man in a Springbok No. 6 shirt that day, Nelson Mandela, who epitomised what the win meant to a changing country. The president's unbridled joy at the final whistle provided the lasting memories of an uninspiring final.

Test rugby's only other extra-time match came four years later at Twickenham. South Africa were again involved, this time against Australia in a riveting semi-final at the fourth World Cup. The sides were deadlocked at 18-all before they had to re-group and play on. South Africa went ahead for the first time in the match with a penalty goal kicked by Jannie de Beer early in extra time, but that was cancelled out by one from Matt Burke before the sides changed ends for the third time. Again there had been no tries scored, and again it was a dropped goal seven minutes from the end that was to settle the match. Stephen Larkham, Australia's fly-half, chose the moment to drop his first goal at Test level. His long, speculative, scruffy kick scudded through the air and scraped over the bar to put Australia into their second final.

GREEN VOLVO STOPS PLAY

SUNBURY, MARCH 1996

The current hum that surrounds the London Irish club dates from 1996 when, as a second division side, two strong personalities, Clive Woodward the coach and Gary Halpin the captain, stamped their mark on a team that began to play expansive rugby. Strong running backs and competitive forwards provided the momentum that drove the club to the top of the table and promotion to the top flight of English rugby.

The 1995–6 season was also memorable as it saw London Irish's best Cup run since their appearance in the 1980 final when they were beaten by Leicester. The Tigers were again their opponents at Sunbury in March 1996 when the clubs were drawn to meet in the semi-finals.

A capacity crowd was in attendance to set both a gate record and a Guinness consumption record for the club. London Irish boldly set out to play their wide game, making no concessions to the forward power of the renowned Leicester forwards. Although the Tigers were ahead 22–8 after only 27 minutes, the storming play of Rob Henderson and the effective goal kicking of Michael Corcoran brought the Irish back into the game and by the interval they only trailed by the slim margin of one point with the score at 21–22.

Then, five minutes into the second half, the concentration of the London Irish team was broken by an event that could only have happened at London Irish. So many had turned up at the ground to watch the match that parking arrangements had been chaotic right up to the time of the kick-off with cars being parked anywhere and everywhere. As the referee prepared to re-start the game with a scrum after a break in play, the public announcement system rumbled into action to request that the owner of a green Volvo, registration number . . . , remove it immediately otherwise the police would do so.

As the scrum was about to go down, Gary Halpin, at tight head prop, held the front rows up. The tannoy message had suddenly sunk in: that green Volvo belonged to none other than the London Irish skipper himself. Play had to be held up while he ambled across the pitch to the dressing room, where he recovered his car keys and gave them to a friend so that the car could be moved.

Unfortunately, the poor Irish never recovered after that, and Leicester raced 46–21 ahead and into a Cup final against Bath.

CROSS CODE CHALLENGE

TWICKENHAM, MAY 1996

A meeting of the Rugby Football Union (RFU) on 19 September 1895 outlawed professionalism in any form and adopted strict new by-laws to govern the structure of the amateur rugby union game. These laws were framed as a reaction to a number of clubs in the north of England who had met two months earlier to vote for a breakaway and formation of what was then known as the Northern Union and which became the rugby league. The main plank of the newly formed organisation's constitution was that a six shilling (30 pence) broken time payment would be made to compensate players for loss of employment, something which the die-hards of the RFU could not and would not entertain.

The two games went strictly down their own paths for a century except during war-time. On the 14 November 1939, the RFU temporarily lifted the ban so that rugby league and rugby union players could join arms to play in service matches until official matches began again in peacetime. Interestingly, the Scottish Union saw no reason for removing the bar on league men.

There were two cross code challenges during the war, the League XV winning the first match 18–11 at Headingley in January 1943. A year later, in April 1944, another special match arranged by Northern Command in which a Rugby League Selection played a Rugby Union Selection was staged at the league's stronghold, Odsal Stadium in Bradford. The match, again played under the 15-a-side code, attracted more than 18,000 curious spectators and raised over £1,350 for charity. As expected, the strong Union XV went ahead early on and led 10–0 at the interval. The League outfit, however, staged a remarkable comeback in the second half and ran out deserved winners by 15–10.

But it was not until rugby union went open in September 1995 with the introduction of the seamless game that the drawbridge between the two codes permanently came down. To celebrate the end of the 100 years' war between league and union, a pair of interesting and unusual challenge matches involving Bath, the English rugby union champions, and Wigan, their rugby league counterparts, were enacted.

The first leg of the challenge, under rugby league rules, was at Maine Road, Manchester early in May 1996. Former Welsh rugby union international and distinguished league coach, Clive Griffiths, was drafted in to give the Bath boys a crash course in the subtleties of the 13-a-side game. A trial match against the South Wales League XIII was a useful taster for the Union boys who did well to score four tries despite conceding eight.

Then it was up to Manchester for the match against the side that had been the cream of the league game for several years. What Bath had done for modern English club rugby union, Wigan had done for rugby league.

Of course, Bath were smashed to smithereens in what amounted to a massive culture shock. It was 82–6 at the end, Wigan strolling in for 16 tries to one scored by Jon Callard. Wigan's lines of running, superior basic skills and imaginative use of space left a deep impression on the Bath players. 'Wigan are a fantastic side,' said Bath captain Phil de Glanville, reflecting on the pace, power and superior fitness of his opponents after the match. 'We turned up,' was the final word of the Bath director of rugby, John Hall.

When Wigan met Bath in the return match, this time under union rules at Twickenham, the kings of the north had already paraded their skills at the ground as special guests of the organising committee of the annual Middlesex Sevens. The

Sevens tournament was the first time that a rugby league side had set foot on the hallowed turf of RFU headquarters, something that could not possibly have been envisaged even five years earlier. Wigan again displayed their sublime skills and entertained a hugely appreciative crowd, beating Harlequins and Leicester before winning the final against Wasps.

Honour at least was restored in the 15-a-side part of the cross code challenge with Bath winning the Twickenham match by 44–19. Even so, Wigan certainly threw down the gauntlet to the English Union champions. It was felt that they would struggle in the scrums, lineouts and rucks, but bolstered by former exponents of the Union game such as Scott Quinnell, Martin Offiah (who had scored six tries at Maine Road) and Inga Tuigamala (who began the match as a flanker), and to a lesser extent, by some sympathetic refereeing from Brian Campsall, the northern champions managed three sparkling tries.

ENGLAND'S WORST HALF-HOUR

TWICKENHAM, MARCH 1997

English supporters had never seen anything like the last 30 minutes of the Twickenham Five Nations match against France on St David's Day, 1997 – not in 129 years covering 475 international matches since 1871.

England, after conceding an early penalty goal in the third minute of the match, were up and in the faces of the French almost from the word go. For the first hour the forwards joined the backs in the 15-man game that coach Jack Rowell preferred to call inter-active rugby as England swept all before them.

The boot of Paul Grayson put England ahead in the first half. The Northampton fly half kicked three penalties to give them a 9–3 advantage after only a dozen minutes and though Christophe Lamaison pulled back three points with a dropped goal for France, Lawrence Dallaglio scored with a 30-metre dash on the stroke of half-time. That score, England's high moment of the match, stretched England into a 14–6 lead that became 20–6 after two more Paul Grayson penalties in the first ten minutes of the second half. 'Swing Low' sang the crowd, anticipating more momentum being generated by its sweet chariot.

But in the last 30 minutes of this vivid match the chariot ground to a halt and eventually lost its wheels. In quite the most extraordinary turn-round ever seen in an England inter-national, Phil de Glanville's men lost the initiative to a French side that began to play with dash. Lamaison was the spark in the backs. Running at the English threequarters, the

Frenchman looked positively dangerous every time he gained possession. Flanker Olivier Magne played with a panache reminiscent of the great Jean-Pierre Rives and was the catalyst in the move that led to France's first try 20 minutes from the end. As play moved to the right the ball came to Lamaison, who dropped a delicate chip into the path of Laurent Leflammand, who gathered it one-handed and swerved outside Tony Underwood for a corner score. Lamaison converted from a difficult angle.

Seven minutes later it was Lamaison who again stormed England's defences after a series of clever French blind-side attacks. His conversion of his own try brought his side level with ten minutes remaining. Then, to cap it all, he kicked the winning penalty three minutes from time making the scoreline 23–20 to France who had scored 17 points without reply while Lamaison had registered the full house of scoring actions: try, conversions and penalties to add to his earlier dropped goal. England had never previously surrendered such a commanding lead.

SIXTY TEST POINTS SCORED AT THE SAME END

DUNEDIN, AUGUST 1997

The Tri Nations tournament launched in 1996 derived from the negotiations that South African, New Zealand and Australian rugby representatives had with Rupert Murdoch's NewsCorp television executives at the time of the 1995 Rugby World Cup. In return for £360 million, the three southern hemisphere powers confirmed that they would meet one another home and away on a round-robin basis every season for the following decade, with Murdoch's media interests having sole broadcasting rights to the competition.

The tournament was an instant success. At last the southern powers had a competition to rival the long established European Five Nations, and crowds flocked to see New Zealand walk off with the inaugural title. In winning the 1996 title, the All Blacks had carried off a Grand Slam and were thus seeking back-to-back Grand Slams when, in the following year's competition, they hosted Australia at Dunedin's Carisbrook ground in mid-August.

New Zealand were unstoppable and powered into an unassailable 36–0 lead in the first 40 minutes. They ran in three tries through Taine Randell, Justin Marshall and Christian Cullen and, with Carlos Spencer in deadly form with the boot, everyone thought that the game was over by the interval. Everyone, that is, except the Australian team.

The Wallabies turned round to stage a spirited recovery in a fascinating second half that was partially spoilt by a number of interruptions for penalties. (All told, French official Joel Dumé saw fit to award 38 penalties during the match.) Stephen Larkham (twice), Joe Roff and Ben Tune ripped the New Zealand defence open to cross for tries, but David Knox managed only two conversions to leave the Wallabies still a dozen points short of the All Blacks, despite outscoring them on tries.

The final result was 36–24 to New Zealand but the scoreline provided the statisticians with the oddity that all sixty of the points gained in the Test match had been registered at the same end of the ground.

FASTEST TEST TRY

MURRAYFIELD, FEBRUARY 1999

In 1923 at Twickenham, Wales had conceded the then fastest
try scored in Test history when Leo Price touched down for
England ten seconds after the kick-off. The record that no-one
believed could be beaten stood for more than 76 years until
Wales, again, conceded an even quicker one at Murrayfield on
the opening day of the last ever Five Nations tournament.

Duncan Hodge lined up as if to take an orthodox kick-off for
Scotland with his forwards in scrum formation to his right. As
the referee blew his whistle to signal the start of the match,
Hodge switched direction and angled the ball to the less
densely populated left where only Matthew Robinson and
Shane Howarth were in position for Wales. Howarth moved
ahead of Robinson to claim the kick but had not anticipated the
quick reactions of the Scottish left-centre, John Leslie. Leslie,
the son of a former All Blacks captain, swooped for the ball like
a bat out of hell and snatched it from Howarth's grasp and set
off on a run towards the Welsh line. On and on he sprinted as
the Welsh cover, badly caught on the hop, desperately tried to
cut across and atone for its poor organisation at the kick-off.
Leslie loped into the Welsh 22 and finished off crashing over to
the left of the posts.

Most of the sell-out crowd had barely settled in their seats
and Scotland were already five points ahead. In the press box,
journalists frantically looked at their stop watches to clock
Leslie's time. Eight seconds? Nine, ten, eleven . . . It wasn't
really until the BBC had re-run the score several times at the

interval that an accurate fix could be made on the score. The media boys reckoned it had taken Leslie nine seconds to score, clipping Leo Price's run-in by one second and setting a new world record for an international match – one that is never likely to be beaten.

The start of the game set the tempo for the following 79 minutes and 50 seconds. Points came thick and fast before Scotland finished 33–20 winners of a match that yielded six tries. Afterwards, Leslie modestly acknowledged the part played in his try by the rest of the Scottish side. 'We planned to put Matthew Robinson under pressure right from the kick off,' he said, 'so although it was a quick try, it was something we had been working on.'

WET PAINT

Advertising – it's hard to believe today, but only 30 or so years ago a spectator could attend a major international match at Cardiff, Twickenham or any of the world's leading rugby union stadiums and not see a single commercial inside the ground and probably only a handful outside.

Slowly all that changed. First came the advertising boards around the playing area and on the fronts of the stands, and nowadays marking the pitch with the sponsor's logo is all the rage. That started in the southern hemisphere where big corporate backers had their insignia painted onto the playing surface at points and angles strategically chosen to show up on television and so attract the attention of the viewer. This gave prime time advertising at a fraction of the cost of sponsoring a commercial break.

The first company to sponsor the entire Five Nations Championship was Lloyds TSB and it has to be said that their media department did a splendid job informing newspapers and television of the colours and sizes that should be used when displaying the company's logo in its match news and screen coverage.

'The dotted line around the mark indicates the minimum exclusion zone,' ran their guidelines. 'This zone has been designed to ensure that the Lloyds TSB Five Nations mark never appears with other graphic material cluttered around it,' continued the detailed advice to newsprint editors.

Pity that this detailed advice did not extend to the type of paint that should be used, or for how long it should be allowed to dry, or under which weather conditions it was suitable. Such information would have been far more useful as Ireland and their popular hooker, Keith Wood, discovered to the amusement of 55,000 spectators at Lansdowne Road and a multi-million television audience.

The first match for the new sponsors was Ireland's Championship opener with France at Lansdowne Road in 1999. Inevitably, the rain in Dublin that started on the morning of the match continued into the afternoon. The wet ground itself was plenty to contend with, but from an early stage in the match it was obvious that the dye used to colour the sponsor's logo on the region either side of the half-way-line had not dried, causing irritation for players and not a few identification problems for spectators and commentators. As soon as players became trapped on the floor in tackles or rucks the vivid blue and green paint rubbed off on their kit and skin.

Now, at the best of times Keith Wood is a fearsome sight on the field. But the sight of his bald pate, face and jersey smeared in war-paint gave him the look of a wild Indian. At one time early in the first half, after having his face rubbed a bit too vigorously in the offending area, he needed to be towelled down like some messy infant before he was able to resume playing. Certainly never was the old maxim, blue and green should never be seen, more apt.

THE AMAZING COMEBACK

BUENOS AIRES, JUNE 1999

Welsh rugby was on a roll in June 1999. After years in the Test wilderness, their Messiah had appeared in the form of one Graham Henry, a former secondary school headmaster from New Zealand who had been the guiding light behind a successful Auckland side.

Henry took over the reins as Wales coach in the autumn of 1998 and immediately instilled a confidence that had been sadly lacking in Welsh XVs for the best part of 20 years. He began his stewardship with a narrow but honourable defeat at Wembley Stadium against South Africa. A win against Argentina at Llanelli was followed by two disappointing Five Nations defeats against Scotland and Ireland. Then, a couple of changes breathed fire into the lungs of a new Welsh pack which paved the way for a one-point victory against France in Paris. This was Wales's first win in the French capital for 24 years, and the season ended in glory with a record win against Italy and an emotional defeat of England in the last ever Five Nations international.

Henry then took his improving side to Argentina to hone its skills for the upcoming Rugby World Cup. For the first Test, the coach carrying the Welsh team had to negotiate the horrors of Buenos Aires's traffic without the promised police escort. As a result, the team arrived with barely 40 minutes to spare before kick-off.

The start of the match reflected the nature of Wales's journey to the ground, with the Pumas bewildering their guests

297

with an avalanche of early points. No Home Union had ever won a series 2–0 in Argentina and, as Wales slumped 23 points in arrears without scoring a point in the first half-hour, it looked as if they were far from likely to break the record.

There then followed the biggest comeback ever seen in 128 years of international rugby. From 0–23 down, Neil Jenkins, inevitably, put Wales on the board with a penalty before Scott Quinnell made one of his most rousing runs to set up the move from which Dafydd James sprinted in for a morale-boosting try on the stroke of half-time. Jenkins converted to reduce the deficit to 13 points as the sides went into the interval.

It was in the second half that the visitors revealed the character that Henry had built into his side in the short time since he had taken over. Only twelve months earlier Wales had capitulated to South Africa, conceding 96 points. Henry, with only a small number of changes in personnel and little extra talent available, had worked wonders to raise a side that now showed courage and grit against a nation that is renowned for being devilishly difficult to beat in its own back yard.

Yet Wales continued to take the game to the Pumas and in a second half that was a triumph for their pack, Wales scored another 26 points to three by Argentina. Jenkins landed three goals and converted two tries scored from line-outs, the first by Brett Sinkinson and the decisive second one by Chris Wyatt who thundered over near the posts after Allan Bateman and Mark Taylor, the Welsh centres, had made pathfinding runs at the defence.

The previous biggest deficit overcome in a Test before Wales's remarkable effort was when South Africa came back from 5–23 down to beat the All Blacks 24–23 in Durban in the 1998 Tri Nations. Before that the most celebrated comeback was that of the Lions against the New Zealand Maoris at Wellington's Athletic Park in 1993.

The Lions fell 0–20 behind and were lucky not to concede another score before staging a brilliant comeback. It was 3–20 with only fifteen minutes to go when the arrival of Jason Leonard as a replacement in the front row stirred the forwards into action. Ieuan Evans and Rory Underwood reminded onlookers of their world class, running in two sumptuous tries and with the conversions, the Lions were back in contention at 17–20. Gavin Hastings, playing the captain's part, finished the match off with a try which he himself converted eight minutes from time. The final score was Maoris 20, Lions 24.

BROTHER AGAINST BROTHER

WREXHAM, OCTOBER 1999

The controversy regarding players' qualifications to play international rugby came to a head in the Brett Sinkinson and Shane Howarth affairs in the 2000 Six Nations Championship. The two New Zealanders, it transpired, were unable to verify their beliefs that they each had a grandparent of Welsh ancestry. Further genealogical searches showed that two established Scotland players, Peter Walton and the Bristol butcher, David Hilton, had mistakenly believed that their international eligibility derived from a Scottish-born grandparent.

These revelations came barely months after a new International Board law (effective from 1 January 2000) ruled that rugby players could no longer appear for more than one nation, so ending a practice that, thanks to various interpretations, had gone on for more than a century.

Arguably the most striking example of the absurdity of the old eligibility laws was the case of the Bachop brothers, Graeme and Steve. Both half-backs and both New Zealand born, the players had appeared together as scrum-half and fly-half respectively in four Tests for New Zealand against South Africa and Australia in 1994. Graeme went on to finish his New Zealand career with 31 caps, the record for an All Black scrum-half, in 1995 before moving to Japan.

At length, he qualified through residence to play for the Japanese and in 1999 was a key member of their Rugby World Cup squad in Wales. There, Japan's opening pool game was against Samoa at the Racecourse Ground, Wrexham where

Bachop lined up against . . . none another than his brother Steve, by now a regular fly-half in the Pacific Islanders' back division.

Steve was a key member of a side that took the Japanese apart 43–9, but the fact that brother played against brother in an international match will long be a favourite with World Cup rugby quiz masters.

The only other instances of pairs of brothers playing on opposite sides at Test level have also involved New Zealand. At Albany in June 1999, Tana Umaga was on the wing for New Zealand playing against his brother Mike, who was at full-back for Samoa. At the same ground a year later, Pita Alatini (New Zealand) and his sibling Sam (Tonga) actually marked one another lining up as second five-eighths when the All Blacks ran up a 102–0 victory under floodlights.

UPSET OF THE MILLENNIUM

TWICKENHAM, OCTOBER 1999

The northern hemisphere's last rugby season of the millennium generated more surprise Test results than any other in the game's history. There was Italy's astonishing debut in the Six Nations when they beat Scotland, the reigning Five Nations champions, and Ireland ended the longest series of defeats in any Test rugby series when they triumphed against France in Paris for the first time in 28 years. But the match that stands out as the surprise of the season is the New Zealand–France semi-final staged at Twickenham in the Rugby World Cup tournament earlier in the season.

The French had struggled against Canada and Fiji to win their pool games before beating Argentina in a quarter final at Lansdowne Road in Dublin. All roads led to Twickenham for the semis, where Australia disposed of South Africa on the Saturday of a delicious weekend of double headers at the Rugby Football Union's headquarters. Sunday's second semi-final, between New Zealand and France, was considered such a formality that many French supporters didn't even bother to make the visit to London to see their side in action.

After all, only four months earlier in Wellington, the French had been overwhelmed 54–7 by the All Blacks during a tour that was meant to act as a build-up to the World Cup tournament. No, France definitely didn't have a chance in the semi-finals and the French press proclaimed as much, too.

The early stages of the match seemed to support all the pre-match expectations that New Zealand would coast into the finals. The All Blacks efficiently compiled a 17–10 lead by half time and went further ahead through a Jonah Lomu try converted by Andrew Mehrtens four minutes after the interval. 24–10 to New Zealand with 35 minutes to go: it was all over bar the shouting, or so everyone thought.

Then came the most extraordinary rearguard action of the millennium. Christophe Lamaison started the French ball rolling with a couple of neatly executed dropped goals in the sixth and ninth minutes of the second half and suddenly the game took on a different complexion. The French front row were holding up their much vaunted rivals, the French lineout with Abdel Benazzi in commanding form was ruling the set-pieces, and their backs, with nothing to lose now, scented the outside chance of upsetting their famous counterparts.

The French spirit was epitomised by the smallest man on the field, the left wing Christophe Dominici from the Paris club, Stade Français. His mad-cap runs at the New Zealand defence paid the unlikeliest dividends. He turned the All Black defence inside out with his mazy runs and gave inspiration to the other 14 men in blue. Two Lamaison penalties brought the French back to within two points of the All Blacks before, on the quarter hour, Dominici himself scorched over for the try that put France ahead. With their handful of supporters and virtually all of the thousands of neutral spectators firmly behind them, the French lead was one that they would not relinquish. Richard Dourthe and Philippe Bernat-Salles finished off glorious French attacks with tries that Lamaison converted to bring him a personal tally of 28 points in the match and, with seven minutes to go, the most extraordinary of Test transformations had taken the score from 10–24 in New Zealand's favour to 43–24 to France.

Never before had the All Blacks conceded 33 points without reply and certainly never before had they given away 43 points in a Test. The textbook approach of the New Zealanders, with the emphasis on eliminating errors and pressurising opponents until gaps opened up had, in one wonderful half-hour, been superseded by the brilliantly unpredictable approach adopted by the French, who played the games of their lives to win with a display of passion and flair.

For the All Blacks, defeat was hard to bear. Their highly respected coach, John Hart, announced his resignation and an entire nation went into mourning. The defeat was even cited as the root cause of the ruling New Zealand Government's fall at the General Election that took place shortly after the end of the Rugby World Cup.

EUROPEAN FIASCO

LLANELLI, APRIL 2000

It was billed as the most important Welsh club match of all time. Llanelli versus Cardiff at Stradey Park in the quarter-final of the Heineken European Cup.

The match turned into a yawn. A dull game ensued with virtually no passages of back play for the sell-out crowd to savour. Llanelli went through to the semi-finals comfortably, but at a time when senior rugby needed the oxygen of good publicity for its increasingly important new competition, once again an opportunity for promoting the game was spoiled by inefficient administrators.

Mid-way through the first-half the referee Didier Mené of France, who had experienced a difficult time quelling the tempers of two charged-up packs, sent loose forwards Owain Williams (Cardiff) and Ian Boobyer (Llanelli) to the sin-bin after a dust-up. Quite right, too, thought the sizeable audience watching the match on BBC television. After all, only an hour earlier in the other European quarter-final being played that day, Stade Français's New Zealand-born centre, Cliff Mytton, had been dealt similar justice playing against Munster by referee Steve Lander.

The two Welsh forwards had been off the field for five minutes when a fiasco began. There was a break in play during which Monsieur Mené's attention was caught by fourth official Ken Brackston and one of the Heineken tournament's organisers.

The Frenchman was informed that there was no sin-bin in

305

operation in the European competitions and that, while the yellow cards shown to Williams and Boobyer should stand, the players should be reinstated immediately. So, after only five minutes off the field, the two forwards re-joined the fray and the match continued its otherwise uneventful course to half time.

It was during the interval that the farce reached Brian Rix proportions. What about the events over in Munster barely an hour earlier? Munster had piled on nine points during Mytton's absence. If, as now seemed likely, the sin-bin did not apply to the tournament, what would be Stade Français's reaction? Would they demand a replay?

Frantic telephone calls were made to Roger Pickering, head honcho of the European Rugby Committee that oversees the Heineken tournament. He at last cleared up the misunderstandings. In January, it transpired, the European Rugby Committee had taken on board the International Board's recommendations regarding use of the sin-bin. The quarter-finals of the Cup were the first Euro matches to be staged since those guidelines had been issued. Unfortunately, a lack of communication had meant that clubs, referees and tournament organisers were unsure of the yellow-card and sin-bin procedure.

Fortunately, the misunderstanding had no bearing on the outcome of the match. For good measure, Monsieur Mené sent Cardiff flanker Martyn Williams to the sin-bin for the full ten minutes after a second-half offence, but the whole affair did little to inspire public confidence in those who administer professional rugby.

RYAN'S SIX THE BEST

BEDFORD, APRIL 2000

Bedford were the whipping boys of the Allied Dunbar Premiership in 1999–2000. Their first win of the season did not come until April, when they defeated Harlequins, but a week later they were brought back to earth by a Saracens team in which Ryan Constable set a record.

Constable, a former Australian cap, returned from duty with the Aussie Sevens side to play in the Sunday match at Goldington Road. The game also marked Kyran Bracken's first senior start after a long period out of rugby through injury.

Constable was the main beneficiary of Bracken's slick service from the base of the scrum. The Sarries backs ran their hapless opponents into the ground and by half-time the Australian threequarter had already scored a hat-trick of tries as his side ran up a 35–12 lead.

After the break Constable advanced to his record, becoming the first player in League history to score six tries in a first division match with a hat trick in both halves. His tries helped his club to a 57–29 win, though the record-breaker was modest in his post-match summing up. 'I was just on the end of some good lead-up work,' he told the *Watford Observer*'s rugby reporter after the match.

The previous record was five tries set by Kenny Logan while playing for Wasps.

FIFTEEN MINUTES OF FAME

BUCHAREST, APRIL 2000

The Dorchester Gladiators enjoyed their 15 minutes of rugby fame on an Easter tour of Romania in 2000. The occasional team of rugby enthusiasts were visiting Bucharest to distribute toys to an orphanage when, thanks to the intervention of a kindly embassy official, they were invited to play a rugby match against one of the Romanian clubs. The Dorchester party, comprising a lively but unfit group of forty-somethings, jumped at the opportunity of playing what they imagined would be a social match against the locals, with the chance to down a couple of pints of Romanian best afterwards.

Unfortunately, an error in translation led to the Romanians greatly overestimating the quality of their English opponents. As a result, the Dorchester boys arrived for their 11 a.m. kick-off only to find that the venue was the National Stadium, that an expectant crowd of thousands had turned up and that the match was to be broadcast live on Romanian television. Their opponents, moreover, were Romania's crack club side, Steaua Bucharest. The hosts fielded half-a-dozen full international players as well as the captain of the Romanian national side.

'We were a bit suspicious when the hosts offered us a training session the night before,' said lock forward Nigel Jones when the Gladiators returned to Britain. 'Not exactly our style,' he continued, 'we did our pre-match build-up in the bar.'

The Romanians, perhaps confusing the name Gladiators with Saracens or the Barbarians, believed their visitors were packed with England's top professional players, despite attempts from the Dorchester players to explain otherwise.

It was only on the pitch that the truth began to dawn on the Romanians. 'They warmed up like professionals while we stood around smoking cigarettes, knowing we were in for trouble,' one of the Gladiators revealed. Once the match started, Steaua quickly piled on the points before realising that they were involved in a mis-match. Consequently, the hosts eased up for the second half and the final score was 60–17.

The Gladiators' full-back, Dave Scaddon, told reporters: 'They were incredibly fit and all in their 20s. People kept telling us they thought we had done brilliantly under the circumstances.'

A GLANCE INTO THE FUTURE?

CARDIFF AND VOIRON, MAY 2000

As this book went to press two fascinating developments were taking place at different levels and in different countries. Both were rugby news items because of the departures from normal practice that they represented. But both, one suspects, could be seen as trial runs for what will become accepted parts of the game.

In Cardiff, the magnificent new Millennium Stadium has a retractable roof which takes no more than a quarter of an hour to close at a cost of £5. On the 27 May 2000, the Welsh Rugby Union staged the first major representative match ever to be played under cover. The game between a Welsh XV and the French Barbarians took place in a dry environment after there had been heavy rain during the day in Cardiff.

Many people, players included, felt that the roof should have been used during the 1999 Rugby World Cup when Wales and Australia met in a downpour. 'Why use a bus when you have a Ferrari in the garage,' asked Wallaby centre Tim Horan after Australia had skidded through to the semi-finals.

There will no doubt be many such 'under cover' matches played in the Millennium stadium, though the honour of staging the first indoor Test to the new Stadium Australia in Sydney in July 2000, when the special Nelson Mandela international between Australia and South Africa took place.

Meanwhile, in southern France, a perhaps more significant trial took place in May when a regional under-16 final between Grenoble and Seyssins at the Voiron Stadium near Grenoble was played with two referees on the pitch. Grenoble won 29–16 but the positioning of the officials was fascinating. While one referee officiated close to the action the other stood about 25 metres away. As the game moved towards the distant official he became the main adjudicator, and vice versa.

When one official watched the side throwing the ball at the lineout, the other stood ten metres back near the opposite touch line on the offside line of the defending team. For scrums, there was a referee by the side of the scrum half introducing the ball while the other was positioned on the opposite side, again on the offside line of the non-introducing team.

It was at the set-pieces where the effect was most telling. The referees enabled the sides to see the off-side lines clearly while it was reported that only one scrum collapsed. That was when a lock deliberately brought the scrum down, an offence for which he was warned.

Michel Breton, a faithful follower and recorder of the game at all levels in France, passes the final word on this innovation. 'I was very impressed. The game was cleaner and faster; the treachery considerably reduced. It is, maybe, the future solution as far as France is concerned.'

REFEREE PLAYS CHARADES

ALBANY, JUNE 2000

New Zealand's opening Test of their first season of the new millennium was against Tonga at the beautifully appointed North Harbour Stadium at Albany on the outskirts of Auckland. New Zealand were never going to find any difficulty disposing of the rugby challenge made by the islanders, and with a typical show of All Black efficiency the hosts ran up a comfortable 48–0 lead by half-time in front of an appreciative Friday-night crowd.

The All Blacks started the second half exactly where they had left off at the end of the first. Doug Howlett, in his first international having replaced Christian Cullen at the break, scored a try within 23 seconds of taking the field as New Zealand went 55–0 ahead.

Five minutes later, the All Blacks won a lineout in the Tongan 22 where Reuben Thorne took the throw from hooker Mark Hammett and charged towards the line. There a maul developed and several bodies were seen to cross the line. With the ball buried beneath half-a-dozen or so bodies, players, spectators and television viewers anxiously awaited the referee's ruling.

But, instead of making a decision, the English referee, Steve Lander, gave a strange signal. He traced the outline of a rectangle with his hands as if he was taking part in a game of charades. Then he turned towards the stand and addressed Steve Walsh, the noted New Zealand referee: 'Steve, have a look at that one, please.'

It was the first time in a major international match that a referee had called for the back up of the video evidence to form a decision. As in the earlier Super Twelves competition involving the leading provincial outfits of New Zealand, South Africa and Australia, referees were now allowed to appeal to the video back up, but only to help make a decision as to whether a try might have been scored. The answer to Mr Lander's question wasn't long in coming. 'Try, try, fellahs,' he announced, awarding the score to the new New Zealand captain, Todd Blackadder.

Twice more over the same weekend and in different parts of the world the video referee would be called on to adjudge tricky goal line situations. In Brisbane against the Wallabies the next day, Argentina would be denied a try by their number eight, Gonzalo Longo, because the video recording was unable to pick up an angle showing whether or not the Puma had grounded the ball after being driven over the line by his pack. And in Pretoria a couple of hours later, England's Tim Stimpson was denied a penalty try after the video referee, Mark Lawrence of South Africa, was called on by the New Zealand referee, Colin Hawke, to adjudicate on the legality of a tackle made by South Africa's André Vos when Stimpson did not appear to have the ball in his hands.

Again, the ruling was no try, the video referee giving the benefit of the doubt to the defending side. Ironically, Mr Hawke later said that under normal circumstances he would probably have given the try. Video referees are here to stay, but it is to be hoped that in future the officials having to consider these tricky rulings are at least neutral like those officiating on the field.